AAT

AQ2016

Elements of Costing

EXAM KIT

This Exam Kit supports study for the following AAT qualifications:
AAT Foundation Certificate in Accounting – Level 2
AAT Foundation Diploma in Accounting and Business – Level 2
AAT Foundation Certificate in Bookkeeping – Level 2
AAT Foundation Award in Accounting Software – Level 2
AAT Level 2 Award in Accounting Skills to Run Your Business
AAT Foundation Certificate in Accounting at SCQF Level 5

KAPLAN

PUBLISHING

British Library Cataloguing-in-Publication Data

A catalogue record for this book is available from the British Library.

Published by:

Kaplan Publishing UK

Unit 2 The Business Centre

Molly Millar's Lane

Wokingham

Berkshire

RG41 2QZ

ISBN: 978-1-78740-796-1

CONTENTS

Features in this exam kit

In addition to providing a wide ranging bank of real exam style questions, we have also included in this kit:

- unit-specific information and advice on exam technique

- our recommended approach to make your revision for this particular unit as effective as possible.

You will find a wealth of other resources to help you with your studies on the AAT website:

www.aat.org.uk/

Quality and accuracy are of the utmost importance to us so if you spot an error in any of our products, please send an email to mykaplanreporting@kaplan.com with full details, or follow the link to the feedback form in MyKaplan.

Our Quality Co-ordinator will work with our technical team to verify the error and take action to ensure it is corrected in future editions.

UNIT-SPECIFIC INFORMATION

THE EXAM

FORMAT OF THE ASSESSMENT

The assessment will comprise ten independent tasks. Students will be assessed by computer-based assessment.

In any one assessment, students may not be assessed on all content, or on the full depth or breadth of a piece of content. The content assessed may change over time to ensure validity of assessment, but all assessment criteria will be tested over time.

The learning outcomes for this unit are as follows:

	Learning outcome	Weighting
1	Understand the cost recording system within an organisation	20%
2	Use cost recording techniques	60%
3	Provide information on actual and budgeted costs and income	20%
	Total	100%

Time allowed

90 minutes

PASS MARK

The pass mark for all AAT CBAs is 70%.

 Always keep your eye on the clock and make sure you attempt all questions!

DETAILED SYLLABUS

The detailed syllabus and study guide written by the AAT can be found at:

www.aat.org.uk/

INDEX TO QUESTIONS AND ANSWERS

VARIANCES

EXAM TECHNIQUE

- **Do not skip any of the material** in the syllabus.

- **Read each question** *very* carefully.

- **Double-check your answer** before committing yourself to it.

- Answer **every** question – if you do not know an answer to a multiple choice question or true/false question, you don't lose anything by guessing. Think carefully before you **guess**.

- If you are answering a multiple-choice question, **eliminate first those answers that you know are wrong.** Then choose the most appropriate answer from those that are left.

- **Don't panic** if you realise you've answered a question incorrectly. Getting one question wrong will not mean the difference between passing and failing.

Computer-based exams – tips

- Do not attempt a CBA until you have **completed all study material** relating to it.

- On the AAT website there is a CBA demonstration. It is **ESSENTIAL** that you attempt this before your real CBA. You will become familiar with how to move around the CBA screens and the way that questions are formatted, increasing your confidence and speed in the actual exam.

- Be sure you understand how to use the **software** before you start the exam. If in doubt, ask the assessment centre staff to explain it to you.

- Questions are **displayed on the screen** and answers are entered using keyboard and mouse. At the end of the exam, you are given a certificate showing the result you have achieved.

- In addition to the traditional multiple-choice question type, CBAs will also contain **other types of questions**, such as number entry questions, drag and drop, true/false, pick lists or drop down menus or hybrids of these.

- In some CBAs you will have to type in complete computations or written answers.

- You need to be sure you **know how to answer questions** of this type before you sit the exam, through practice.

KAPLAN'S RECOMMENDED REVISION APPROACH

QUESTION PRACTICE IS THE KEY TO SUCCESS

Success in professional examinations relies upon you acquiring a firm grasp of the required knowledge at the tuition phase. In order to be able to do the questions, knowledge is essential.

However, the difference between success and failure often hinges on your exam technique on the day and making the most of the revision phase of your studies.

The **Kaplan Study Text** is the starting point, designed to provide the underpinning knowledge to tackle all questions. However, in the revision phase, poring over text books is not the answer.

Kaplan Pocket Notes are designed to help you quickly revise a topic area; however you then need to practise questions. There is a need to progress to exam style questions as soon as possible, and to tie your exam technique and technical knowledge together.

The importance of question practice cannot be over-emphasised.

The recommended approach below is designed by expert tutors in the field, in conjunction with their knowledge of the examiner and the specimen assessment.

You need to practise as many questions as possible in the time you have left.

OUR AIM

Our aim is to get you to the stage where you can attempt exam questions confidently, to time, in a closed book environment, with no supplementary help (i.e. to simulate the real examination experience).

Practising your exam technique is also vitally important for you to assess your progress and identify areas of weakness that may need more attention in the final run up to the examination.

In order to achieve this we recognise that initially you may feel the need to practice some questions with open book help.

Good exam technique is vital.

KAPLAN PUBLISHING

THE KAPLAN REVISION PLAN

Stage 1: Assess areas of strengths and weaknesses

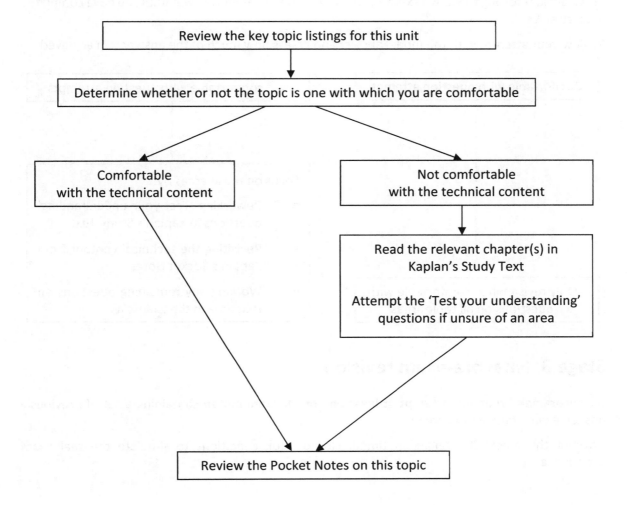

Review the key topic listings for this unit

Determine whether or not the topic is one with which you are comfortable

Comfortable
with the technical content

Not comfortable
with the technical content

Read the relevant chapter(s) in
Kaplan's Study Text

Attempt the 'Test your understanding'
questions if unsure of an area

Review the Pocket Notes on this topic

Stage 2: Practice questions

Follow the order of revision of topics as presented in this Kit and attempt the questions in the order suggested.

Try to avoid referring to Study Texts and your notes and the model answer until you have completed your attempt.

Review your attempt with the model answer and assess how much of the answer you achieved.

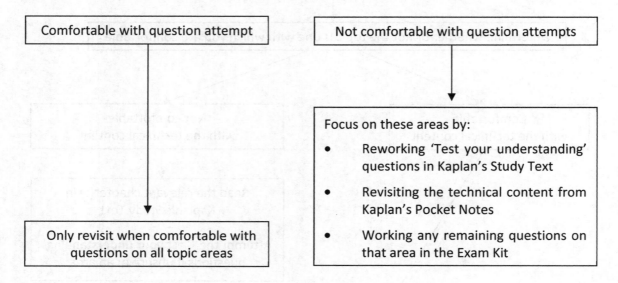

| Comfortable with question attempt | | Not comfortable with question attempts |

Focus on these areas by:

- Reworking 'Test your understanding' questions in Kaplan's Study Text

- Revisiting the technical content from Kaplan's Pocket Notes

- Working any remaining questions on that area in the Exam Kit

Only revisit when comfortable with questions on all topic areas

Stage 3: Final pre-exam revision

We recommend that you **attempt at least one mock examination** containing a set of previously unseen exam-standard questions.

Attempt the mock CBA online in timed, closed book conditions to simulate the real exam experience.

Section 1

PRACTICE QUESTIONS

COST CLASSIFICATION

FINANCIAL AND MANAGEMENT ACCOUNTING

1 FAMA

The table below lists some of the characteristics of financial accounting and management accounting systems.

Indicate two characteristics for each system by putting a tick in the relevant column of the table below:

Characteristic	Financial accounting	Management accounting
• Have to be produced annually.		
• Analyses historic events to help produce forecasts.		
• Is always produced using accounting standards.		
• Is produced on an ad hoc basis when required.		

2 FINANCIAL AND MANAGEMENT

The table below lists some of the characteristics of financial accounting and management accounting systems.

Indicate two characteristics for each system by putting a tick in the relevant column of the table below:

Characteristic	Financial accounting	Management accounting
• Must be presented as specified by the Companies Act and accounting standards.		
• Helps managers run the business on a day-to-day basis.		
• Used as the basis for the calculation of the organisation's tax charge.		
• Can include anything that managers feel is useful for the business.		

3   MAFA

The table below lists some of the characteristics of financial accounting and management accounting systems.

Indicate two characteristics for each system by putting a tick in the relevant column of the table below:

Characteristic	Management accounting	Financial accounting
• It is based on past events.		
• Its purpose is to provide information for managers.		
• It is based on future events.		
• It complies with company law and accounting rules.		

4   FEATURES

The table below lists some features typical of financial accounting and management accounting systems.

Indicate which feature applies to which system by putting a tick in the relevant column of the table below:

Feature	Financial accounting	Management accounting
• Analysis of profit by cost centre.		
• Statement of profit or loss using format as dictated by accounting standards and company law.		
• Cash flow forecasts.		
• Cost per unit calculation.		

COST AND PROFIT CENTRES

5   JEREMY

Jeremy operates a business that bakes bread. These are made in a small bakery and then sent to Jeremy's shop, where they are sold. Jeremy also has a small office where all of the administration is undertaken.

Identify whether the following departments are likely to be profit or cost centres by putting a tick in the relevant column of the table below:

Department	Cost centre	Profit centre
• Bakery		
• Shop		
• Office		

6   PRINT PLC

Print plc is a large company that prints and sells books. It is split into three divisions – binding, shops and marketing. The binding department prints the books. These are then either transferred to Print's chain of shops where they are sold to the public, or sold direct from the binding department to corporate clients. The marketing department produces all of Print's advertising.

Identify whether the following departments are likely to be profit or cost centres by putting a tick in the relevant column of the table below:

Department	Cost centre	Profit centre
• Binding		
• Shops		
• Marketing		

7   HOOCH PLC

Identify whether the following definitions are of be profit, cost, or investment centres by putting a tick in the relevant column of the table below:

Department	Cost centre	Profit centre	Investment centre
• Hooch's manager has no responsibility for income or asset purchases and disposals.			
• Hooch's manager is assessed on the profitability of their department, as well as how effectively they have controlled their assets.			
• Hooch's manager is responsible for income and expenditure of their department only.			

CLASSIFYING COSTS BY ELEMENT (MATERIALS, LABOUR OR OVERHEADS)

8   VVV LTD

VVV Ltd manufactures toy planes.

Classify the following costs by element (materials, labour or overheads) by putting a tick in the relevant column of the table below:

Cost	Materials	Labour	Overheads
• Paint used on the planes.			
• Depreciation of the machines used in the factory.			
• Oil used on the machines in the factory.			
• Salary of worker assembling the planes.			

9   TRIP LTD

Trip Ltd is a company that provides travel insurance.

Classify the following costs by element (materials, labour or overheads) by putting a tick in the relevant column of the table below:

Cost	Materials	Labour	Overheads
• Wages of the insurance clerks dealing with claims.			
• Rent of the office.			
• Paper used to print off insurance policies.			
• Salary of the office manager.			

10   FRUWT LTD

FRUWT Ltd manufactures and sells fruit juice.

Classify the following costs by element (materials, labour or overheads) by putting a tick in the relevant column of the table below:

Cost	Materials	Labour	Overheads
• Purchase of fruit for juicing.			
• Electricity used by juicing machines.			
• Water added to the juice before sale.			
• Wages of staff operating juicing machinery.			

11   MARTINA

Martina provides legal services in her home town.

Classify the following costs by element (materials, labour or overheads) by putting a tick in the relevant column of the table below:

Cost	Materials	Labour	Overheads
• Stationery used in Martina's court cases.			
• Wages of Martina's secretary.			
• Water rates for Martina's office.			
• Cost of training courses taken by Martina.			

CLASSIFYING COSTS BY NATURE (DIRECT OR INDIRECT)

12 KHALED

Khaled runs a newspaper.

Classify the following costs by nature (direct or indirect) by putting a tick in the relevant column of the table below:

Cost	Direct	Indirect
• Paper used in the newspapers.		
• Wages of warehouse staff.		
• Heat and light for head office.		
• Ink used in printing the newspapers.		

13 RUSSETT LTD

Russett Ltd is in business as a tablet computer manufacturer.

Classify the following costs by nature (direct or indirect) by putting a tick in the relevant column of the table below:

Cost	Direct	Indirect
• Glass used to make tablets.		
• Insurance of factory.		
• Wages of workers assembling tablets.		
• Cost of entertaining corporate clients.		

14 SCOTLAND LTD

Scotland Ltd makes sports clothing.

Classify the following costs by nature (direct or indirect) by putting a tick in the relevant column of the table below:

Cost	Direct	Indirect
• Cleaners' wages.		
• Advertising expense.		
• Material used in production.		
• Production manager's wages.		
• Machinist wages.		

15 DIRECT OR INDIRECT

Classify the following costs by nature (direct or indirect) by putting a tick in the relevant column of the table below:

Cost	Direct	Indirect
• Chargeable hour for a lawyer.		
• Machine hire for a building contractor in a long term contract.		
• Electricity for a garden centre.		
• Audit fee for a restaurant.		

16 DIRECT COSTS

Direct costs are conventionally deemed to:

A   be constant in total when activity levels alter

B   be constant per unit of activity

C   vary per unit of activity where activity levels alter

D   vary in total when activity levels remain constant

CLASSIFYING COSTS BY FUNCTION (PRODUCTION, ADMINISTRATION OR SELLING AND DISTRIBUTION)

17 NOOGLE LTD

Noogle Ltd produces microwaveable ready meals.

Classify the following costs by function (production, administration, or selling and distribution) by putting a tick in the relevant column of the table below:

Cost	Production	Administration	Selling and distribution
• Purchases of plastic for ready meal containers.			
• Depreciation of sales department's delivery lorries.			
• Insurance of office computers.			
• Salaries of production workers.			

18   HEAVING LTD

Heaving Ltd produces exercise equipment.

Classify the following costs by function (production, administration, or selling and distribution) by putting a tick in the relevant column of the table below:

Cost	Production	Administration	Selling and distribution
• Paper used to print off sales invoices.			
• Metal used to make weights and bars.			
• Depreciation of sales person's vehicle.			
• Repairs to machine in factory.			

19   KORMA PLC

Classify the following costs by function (production, administration, selling and distribution or finance) by putting a tick in the relevant column of the table below:

Cost	Production	Administration	Selling and distribution	Finance
• Direct materials.				
• Sales director salary.				
• Head office printer ink.				
• Direct labour.				
• Bank charges.				

20   JAMES

James makes false teeth.

Classify the following costs by function (production, administration, selling and distribution or finance) by putting a tick in the relevant column of the table below:

Cost	Production	Administration	Selling and distribution	Finance
• Salary of receptionist.				
• Plastic used in false teeth.				
• Stationery provided to all departments.				
• Interest on James' bank overdraft.				
• Electricity for James' factory.				

CLASSIFYING COSTS BY BEHAVIOUR (FIXED, VARIABLE OR SEMI-VARIABLE)

21 QUARK LTD

Quark Ltd runs a bar.

Classify the following costs by their behaviour (fixed, variable, or semi-variable) by putting a tick in the relevant column of the table below:

Cost	Fixed	Variable	Semi-variable
• Bar manager's salary.			
• Alcohol used to make drinks.			
• Rent of bar.			
• Telephone costs, including standard line rental charge.			

22 MORN LTD

Morn Ltd is a manufacturer of chairs and stools.

Classify the following costs by their behaviour (fixed, variable, or semi-variable) by putting a tick in the relevant column of the table below:

Cost	Fixed	Variable	Semi-variable
• Wood used in production.			
• Advertising manager's salary.			
• Electricity costs which include a standing charge.			
• Labour costs paid on a piecework basis.			

23 STEPPED FIXED COST

Which of the following would usually be classed as a stepped fixed cost?

A   Supervisor's wages

B   Raw materials

C   Rates

D   Telephone

24 BRAETAK LTD

Classify the following costs by their behaviour (fixed, variable, or semi-variable) by putting a tick in the relevant column of the table below:

Cost	Fixed	Variable	Semi-variable
• Rent of an office building.			
• Wages of production staff paid on an hourly basis.			
• Wages of production staff paid by a piece rate method.			
• Sales staff paid a basic wage plus commission for each unit sold.			

25 ODO LTD

Odo Ltd is a manufacturer of clothes.

Classify the following costs by their behaviour (fixed, variable, or semi-variable) by putting a tick in the relevant column of the table below:

Cost	Fixed	Variable	Semi-variable
• Material used in the production process.			
• Safety review fee for the year.			
• Electricity costs which include a standing charge.			
• Labour costs paid on a per unit basis.			

26 DEFINITIONS

Identify the following costs by their behaviour (fixed, variable, or semi-variable) by putting a tick in the relevant column of the table below:

Behaviour	Fixed	Variable	Semi-variable	Stepped cost
• This type of cost increases in direct proportion to the amount of units produced.				
• This type of cost has a fixed and a variable element.				
• This type of cost remains constant despite changes in output.				
• This type of cost is fixed within a certain range of output.				

27 MATCH A GRAPH

Match a graph to each of the following costs by labelling each graph with a letter (A–E):

(a)   Variable cost per unit

(b)   Total fixed cost

(c)   Stepped fixed costs

(d)   Total variable cost

(e)   Semi-variable cost

Note: Each graph may relate to more than one cost.

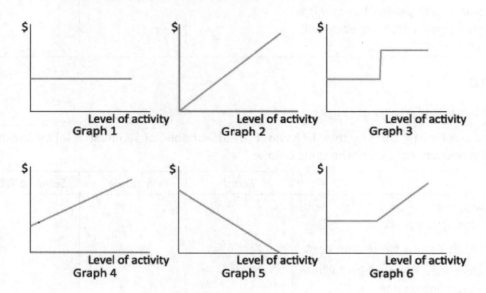

COST CODING

28 BYTES LTD

Bytes Limited operates an IT consultancy business and uses a coding system for its elements of cost (materials, labour or overheads) and then further classifies each element by nature (direct or indirect cost) as below:

So, for example, the code for direct materials is A100.

Element of cost	Code	Nature of cost	Code
Materials	A	Direct	100
		Indirect	200
Labour	B	Direct	100
		Indirect	200
Overheads	C	Direct	100
		Indirect	200

Code the following costs, extracted from invoices and payroll, using the table below:

Cost	Code
• Salary of trainee IT consultant. • Planning costs to renew lease of the office. • Wages of the office manager. • Cleaning materials used by cleaner.	

29 HERO LTD

Hero Ltd, a manufacturer of superhero costumes, uses a numerical coding structure based on one profit centre and three cost centres as outlined below. Each code has a sub-code so each transaction will be coded as ***/***

Profit/cost centre	Code	Sub-classification	Sub-code
Sales	115	Women's costumes	085
		Men's costumes	095
Production	225	Direct cost	110
		Indirect cost	115
Administration	485	Direct cost	220
		Indirect cost	230
Selling and distribution	760	Direct cost	320
		Indirect cost	340

Code the following revenue and expense transactions, which have been extracted from purchase invoices, sales invoices and payroll, using the table below:

Transaction	Code
• Cost of major advertising campaign. • Oil for machinery in factory. • Silk used in manufacturing of costumes. • Insurance of head office. • Sale of women's costumes to a supermarket chain. • Wages paid to delivery van drivers.	

30   VILLAIN LTD

Villain Ltd, a mining company, uses a numerical coding structure based on one profit centre and three cost centres as outlined below. Each code has a sub-code so each transaction will be coded as ***/***

Profit/cost centre	Code	Sub-classification	Sub-code
Revenue	011	Gold sales	100
		Other sales	200
Production	015	Direct Cost	100
		Indirect Cost	200
Administration	019	Direct Cost	100
		Indirect Cost	200
Selling and distribution	024	Direct Cost	100
		Indirect Cost	200

Code the following revenue and expense transactions, which have been extracted from purchase invoices, sales invoices and payroll, using the table below:

Transaction	Code
• Petrol used to run drilling machinery.	
• Sale of silver to a jewellery manufacturer.	
• Replacement of worn out drilling machinery parts.	
• Depreciation of fleet of delivery lorries.	
• Salary of finance director.	
• Sale of gold to an electronics company.	

31   NAYULZ LTD

Nayulz Limited operates a chain of nail salons across Europe and America.

Code the following transactions for the project, using the table below. Each transaction should have a five-character code.

Activity	Code	Nature of cost	Sub-code
Investments	IN	External	100
		Internal	110
Revenues	RE	Europe	225
		America	228
Costs	CO	Material	315
		Labour	318
		Overheads	325

Code the following costs, extracted from invoices and payroll, using the table below:

Cost	Code
• Income earned from salons in New York City, America. • Bank loans raised to open a new store in London. • Nail polish purchased for use in salon. • Heat and light for salon. • Nayulz funds invested in new project.	

32 JUMPER LTD

Jumper Ltd manufactures a range of different items of clothing, which it sells to various types of organisation.

The company analyses sales using an alphanumeric coding system depending on the type of clothing being sold, as well as the type of organisation the clothes are being sold to.

Type of clothing	Code
Trousers	TRS
Jumpers	KNI
Coats	MCN

Sale made to:	Code
Individuals	315
Shops	425
Offices	515
Factories	635

For example, sale of coats to a factory would be coded as MCN/635

Code the following transactions, using the table below:

Sale	Code
• Sale of one jumper to Mrs S. Wooley. • Sale of protective trousers to a factory in London. • Sale of large coats to an office in Birmingham. • Sale of woolen jumpers to a shop in Halifax. • Sale of four coats to Mr A. West. • Sale of three hundred trousers to a shop in Manchester.	

33   GREENFINGERS

Greenfingers Ltd runs a garden centre and uses a coding system for its transactions.

Code the following transactions, using the table below. Each transaction must have a five character code.

Element of cost	Code	Nature of cost	Code
Investments	IN	External	515
		Internal	615
Revenues	RV	Plants	770
		Other	795
Costs	CS	Material	880
		Labour	890
		Overheads	900

Code the following costs, extracted from invoices and payroll, using the table below:

Cost	Code
• Purchase of seeds used to grow plants for resale.	
• External loans for investment in new greenhouses.	
• Wages of gardeners who maintain the plants to be sold.	
• Sales of food and drink.	

COST BEHAVIOUR

CALCULATION QUESTIONS

34   HULK PLC

Identify the type of cost behaviour (fixed, variable or semi-variable) described in each statement by putting a tick in the relevant column of the table below:

Statement	Fixed	Variable	Semi-variable
• Costs are £37,500 when 7,500 units are made and £62,500 when 12,500 units are made.			
• Costs are £2 per unit when 7,500 units are made and £1.20 per unit when 12,500 units are made.			
• Costs are £50,000 when 7,500 units are made and £80,000 when 12,500 units are made.			

35 BANNER PLC

Identify the type of cost behaviour (fixed, variable or semi-variable) described in each statement by putting a tick in the relevant column of the table below:

Statement	Fixed	Variable	Semi-variable
• Costs are £5,000 plus £45 per unit, regardless of the number of units made.			
• Costs are £5,000 when 300 units are made and £5,000 when 600 units are made.			
• Costs are £35 per unit regardless of the number of units made.			

36 NORTON PLC

Identify the type of cost behaviour (fixed, variable or semi-variable) described in each statement by putting a tick in the relevant column of the table below:

Statement	Fixed	Variable	Semi-variable
• Costs are £50,000 in total regardless of the number of units made.			
• Costs are £50,000 in total when 2,500 units are made and £80,000 when 4,000 units are made.			
• Costs are £7 per unit when 1,000 units are made and £6 per unit when 2,000 units are made.			

37   TRIUMPH LTD

Task 1

Identify the type of cost behaviour (fixed, variable or semi-variable) described in each statement by ticking the relevant boxes in the table below.

Statement	Fixed	Variable	Semi-variable
At 9,000 units this cost is £29,250, and at 12,000 units it is £39,000			
At 5,000 units this cost is £5.20 per unit, and at 8,000 units it is £3.25 per unit			
At 19,800 units, this cost is £64,500, and at 27,000 units it is £82,500			

Task 2

Complete the table below by inserting all costs for activity levels of 6,000 and 14,000.

	6,000 units	7,000 units	10,000 units	14,000 units
Variable cost (£)				
Fixed cost (£)				
Total cost (£)		45,000	54,000	

38   YOUNGS LTD

Task 1

Identify the type of cost behaviour (fixed, variable or semi-variable) described in each statement by ticking the relevant boxes in the table below.

Statement	Fixed	Variable	Semi-variable
At 4,000 units this cost is £3.00 per unit, and at 6,000 units it is £2.00 per unit.			
At 7,000 units this cost is £32,500, and at 10,000 units it is £43,000.			
At 11,000 units this cost is £57,750, and at 15,000 units it is £78,750.			

Task 2

Complete the table below by inserting all costs for activity levels of 8,000 and 16,000.

	8,000 units	10,000 units	13,000 units	16,000 units
Variable cost (£)				
Fixed cost (£)				
Total cost (£)		60,500	73,250	

39   CARE PLC

Task 1

Identify the type of cost behaviour (fixed, variable or semi-variable) described in each statement by ticking the relevant boxes in the table below.

Statement	Fixed	Variable	Semi-variable
At 8,000 units this cost is £38,000, and at 12,000 units it is £49,000			
At 10,500 units this cost is £39,375, and at 14,000 units it is £52,500			
At 4,000 units this cost is £4.50 per unit, and at 6,000 units is £3.00 per unit			

Task 2

Complete the table below by inserting all costs for activity levels of 3,000 and 12,000.

	3,000 units	5,000 units	9,000 units	12,000 units
Variable cost (£)				
Fixed cost (£)				
Total cost (£)		13,000	19,800	

40   ROBSHAW LTD

Task 1

Identify the type of cost behaviour (fixed, variable or semi-variable) described in each statement by ticking the relevant boxes in the table below.

Statement	Fixed	Variable	Semi-variable
At 6,000 units this cost is £3.75 per unit, and at 9,000 units it is £2.50 per unit			
At 8,500 units this cost is £36,550, and at 11,300 units it is £48,590			
At 11,000 units this cost is £27,750, and at 14,000 units it is £33,000			

Task 2

Complete the table below by inserting all costs for activity levels of 9,000 and 16,500.

	9,000 units	11,000 units	14,000 units	16,500 units
Variable cost (£)				
Fixed cost (£)				
Total cost (£)		40,250	50,000	

NARRATIVE STYLE QUESTIONS

41   BUNGLE LTD

Bungle Ltd usually produces 9,000 units but is planning to increase production to 14,000 units during the next period.

Identify the following statements as either true or false by putting a tick in the relevant column of the table below:

Statement	True	False
• Total variable costs will decrease.		
• Total fixed costs will remain the same.		
• The variable cost per unit will remain the same.		
• The fixed cost per unit will increase.		

42   TF

Identify the following statements as either true or false by putting a tick in the relevant column of the table below:

Statement	True	False
• Variable costs change directly with changes in activity.		
• Fixed costs change directly with changes in activity.		
• Stepped costs are fixed within a set range of output.		

43   FIXED OR VARIABLE

Identify the following costs as either fixed or variable by putting a tick in the relevant column of the table below:

Cost	Fixed	Variable
• Direct materials.		
• Power used in production machinery.		
• Training costs for new employees in production.		
• Insurance for sales cars.		
• Insurance for machinery.		
• Sales commission.		

44   FOV

Identify the following costs as either fixed or variable by putting a tick in the relevant column of the table below:

Cost	Fixed	Variable
• Piecework wages paid to factory workers.		
• Salaries paid to company directors.		
• Annual payment for cleaning of air conditioning units.		

45   VOF

VOF is a company that prints magazines and newspapers.

Identify the following costs as either fixed or variable by putting a tick in the relevant column of the table below:

Cost	Fixed	Variable
• Annual salaries paid to factory managers.		
• Hourly wages paid to factory workers.		
• Colour ink used to print magazines.		

46   STORM

Indicate whether each of the following costs is an overhead or not by putting a tick in the relevant column of the table below:

	Overhead?	
Cost	Yes	No
• Labour cost of workers who assemble the product.		
• Insurance cost of factory where product is assembled.		
• Electricity for machinery.		

47   ROGUE

Indicate whether each of the following costs is an overhead or not by putting a tick in the relevant column of the table below:

	Overhead?	
Cost	Yes	No
• Labour cost of cleaning staff in a factory.		
• Depreciation of delivery vans.		
• Cost of materials used to build the product.		

48   GAMBIT

Indicate whether each of the following costs is an overhead or not by putting a tick in the relevant column of the table below:

	Overhead?	
Cost	Yes	No
• Wages of staff paid on a piecework system. • Cost of factory canteen staff hourly wages. • Direct materials.		

COST CARDS, TOTAL COSTS AND UNIT COSTS

49   JEEPERS LTD

Indicate whether the following costs are direct or not by putting a tick in the relevant column of the table below:

Cost	Yes	No
• Materials used in production. • Piecework labour costs. • Salary of chief executive.		

Jeepers Ltd makes a single product. At a production level of 15,000 units, the company has the following costs:

Materials	37,500 kilos at £14.00 per kilo
Labour	7,500 hours at £16.00 per hour
Overheads	£570,000

Complete the table below to show the unit product cost at the production level of 15,000 units. Overheads are absorbed on a cost per unit basis. Give your answer to the nearest pound.

Element	Unit product cost
Materials	£
Labour	£
Direct cost	£
Overheads	£
Total	£

50 BRANIAC LTD

Braniac Ltd makes a single product. A production level of 55,000 units has the following costs:

Materials	96,250 litres at £14 per litre
Labour	192,500 hours at £11.50 per hour
Overheads	£687,500

Complete the following unit cost table for a production level of 55,000 units. Overheads are absorbed on a cost per unit basis. Give your answer to the nearest penny.

Element	Unit cost
Materials	£
Labour	£
Direct cost	£
Overheads	£
Total	£

51 GLORIA LTD

Gloria Ltd is costing a single product which has the following cost details:

Variable costs per unit

Materials	£2
Labour	£3
Royalties	£0.50

Total fixed costs

Production overhead	£80,000
Sales and distribution	£90,000

Complete the following total cost and unit cost table for a production level of 20,000 units. Give your answer to the nearest penny for the unit cost and the nearest pound for the total cost.

Element	Unit cost	Total cost for 20,000 units
Variable production costs	£	£
Fixed production costs	£	£
Total production cost	£	£

52 BIZARRO LTD

Bizarro Ltd makes a single product and for a production level of 17,000 units has the following cost details:

	Per unit	Cost
Materials	2.5kg	£18/kilo
Labour	1.0hrs	£9/hour
Fixed overheads		£42,500

Complete the table below to show the unit cost and total cost at the production level of 17,000 units. Overheads are absorbed on a cost per unit basis. Give your answer to the nearest penny for the unit cost and the nearest pound for total cost.

Element	Unit cost	Total cost
Materials	£	£
Labour	£	£
Overheads	£	£
Total	£	£

53 VINNY LTD

Vinny Ltd is a commercial laundrette below are the costings for 15,000 units:

Variable costs

Materials £75,000

Labour £120,000

Fixed costs

Production overhead £100,000

Complete the following total cost and unit cost table for a REVISED production level of 20,000 units. Give your answer to the nearest penny for the unit cost and the nearest pound for total cost.

Element	Unit cost	Total cost
Materials	£	£
Labour	£	£
Overheads	£	£
Total	£	£

54 DARKSEID LTD

Darkseid Ltd makes a single product and for a production level of 95,000 units has the following cost details:

Materials	47,500kg	at £7/kilo
Labour	71,250hrs	at £9/hour
Fixed overheads		£242,000

Complete the table below to show the unit cost at a REVISED production level of 100,000 units. Overheads are absorbed on a cost per unit basis. Give your answer to the nearest penny.

Element	Unit cost
Materials	£
Labour	£
Fixed overheads	£
Total	£

55   DOOMSDAY LTD

Doomsday Ltd is costing a single product which has the following cost details:

Variable costs per unit	Per unit	Cost
Materials	45kg	£0.50/kg
Labour	2.5hrs	£16/hour

Total fixed costs

Production overhead	£75,000
Administration overhead	£110,000
Sales and distribution	£75,000

Complete the following total cost and unit cost table for a production level of 20,000 units. Overheads are absorbed on a cost per unit basis. Give your answer to the nearest penny for the unit cost and the nearest pound for total cost.

Element	Total cost for 20,000 units	Unit cost
Direct costs	£	£
Production overhead	£	£
Non production overhead	£	£
Total costs	£	£

56   OLSEN LTD

Olsen Ltd is costing a single product which has the following cost details:

Variable costs	Per unit
Materials	£12
Labour	£17

Total Fixed Costs

Production overhead	£80,000
Administration overhead	£40,000

Complete the following total cost and unit cost table for a production level of 80,000 units. Give your answer to the nearest penny for the unit cost and the nearest pound for total cost.

Element	Total cost	Unit cost
Materials	£	£
Labour	£	£
Production overheads	£	£
Administration overheads	£	£
Total	£	£

57   FLAKEWAY LTD

Flakeway Ltd makes a single product and for a production level of 24,000 units has the following cost details:

Materials	6,000kg	at £20/kilo
Labour	8,000hrs	at £12/hour
Fixed overheads		£48,000

Complete the table below to show the unit cost at the production level of 24,000 units. Overheads are absorbed on a cost per unit basis. Give your answer to the nearest penny.

Element	Unit cost
Materials	£
Labour	£
Fixed overheads	£
Total	£

58   CORONATION LTD

Coronation Ltd is costing a single product which has the following cost details

Variable costs	Per unit	Cost
Materials	50g	£10/kg
Labour	1hr	£6/hour

Total fixed costs

Production overhead	£40,000
Administration overhead	£20,000
Sales and distribution	£25,000

Complete the following total cost and unit cost table for a production level of 5,000 units. Overheads are absorbed on a cost per unit basis. Give your answer to the nearest penny for the unit cost and the nearest pound for total cost.

Element	Total cost for 5,000 units	Unit cost
Direct costs	£	£
Production overhead	£	£
Non production overhead	£	£
Total costs	£	£

59   LUTHOR LTD

Luthor Ltd makes a single product and for a production level of 15,000 units has the following cost details:

Materials	60,000kg	at £15/kilo
Labour	37,500hrs	at £9/hour
Fixed overheads		£570,000

Complete the table below to show the unit cost at the production level of 15,000 units. Overheads are absorbed on a cost per unit basis. Give your answer to the nearest penny.

Element	Unit cost
Materials	£
Labour	£
Fixed overheads	£
Total	£

60   WILKINSON LTD

Wilkinson Ltd is looking to calculate the unit cost for one of the products it makes. It needs to calculate an overhead absorption rate to apply to each unit. The methods it is considering are a rate per machine hour, a rate per labour hour, and a rate per unit.

Total factory activity is forecast as follows:

Machine hours	10,000
Labour hours	12,500
Units	60,000
Overheads	£150,000

Task 1

Complete the table below to show the possible overhead absorption rates that Wilkinson Ltd could use. The absorption rates should be calculated to two decimal places.

	Machine hour	Labour hour	Unit
Overheads (£)			
Activity			
Absorption rate (£)			

Task 2

The following data relates to making one unit of the product:

Material	2 kilos at £5 per kilo
Labour	15 minutes at £10 per hour
Production time	10 minutes

Complete the table below (to two decimal places) to calculate the total unit cost, using the three overhead absorption rates you have calculated in task 1.

Cost	Machine hour (£)	Labour hour (£)	Unit (£)
Material			
Labour			
Direct cost			
Overheads			
Total unit cost			

61 HODGSON LTD

Hodgson Ltd is looking to calculate the unit cost for one of the products it makes. It needs to calculate an overhead absorption rate to apply to each unit. The methods it is considering are a rate per machine hour, a rate per labour hour, and a rate per unit.

Total factory activity is forecast as follows:

Machine hours	15,000
Labour hours	20,000
Units	100,000
Overheads	£250,000

Task 1

Complete the table below to show the possible overhead absorption rates that Hodgson Ltd could use. The absorption rates should be calculated to two decimal places.

	Machine hour	Labour hour	Unit
Overheads (£)			
Activity			
Absorption rate (£)			

Task 2

The following data relates to making one unit of the product:

Material	4 kilos at £6 per kilo
Labour	30 minutes at £12 per hour
Production time	20 minutes

Complete the table below (to two decimal places) to calculate the total unit cost, using the three overhead absorption rates you have calculated in task 1.

Cost	Machine hour (£)	Labour hour (£)	Unit (£)
Material			
Labour			
Direct cost			
Overheads			
Total unit cost			

62   BARNES LTD

Barnes Ltd is looking to calculate the unit cost for one of the products it makes. It needs to calculate an overhead absorption rate to apply to each unit. The methods it is considering are a rate per machine hour, a rate per labour hour, and a rate per unit.

Total factory activity is forecast as follows:

Machine hours	17,500
Labour hours	12,000
Units	40,000
Overheads	£130,000

Task 1

Complete the table below to show the possible overhead absorption rates that Barnes Ltd could use. The absorption rates should be calculated to two decimal places.

	Machine hour	Labour hour	Unit
Overheads (£)			
Activity			
Absorption rate (£)			

Task 2

The following data relates to making one unit of the product:

Material	3 kilos at £5 per kilo
Labour	20 minutes at £15 per hour
Production time	30 minutes

Complete the table below (to two decimal places) to calculate the total unit cost, using the three overhead absorption rates you have calculated in task 1.

Cost	Machine hour (£)	Labour hour (£)	Unit (£)
Material			
Labour			
Direct cost			
Overheads			
Total unit cost			

63   MAJA LTD

Maja Ltd is looking to calculate the unit cost for one of the products it makes. It needs to calculate an overhead absorption rate to apply to each unit. The methods it is considering are a rate per machine hour, a rate per labour hour, and a rate per unit.

Total factory activity is forecast as follows:

Machine hours	9,000
Labour hours	11,000
Units	60,000
Overheads	£145,000

Task 1

Complete the table below to show the possible overhead absorption rates that Maja Ltd could use. The absorption rates should be calculated to two decimal places.

	Machine hour	Labour hour	Unit
Overheads (£)			
Activity			
Absorption rate (£)			

Task 2

The following data relates to making one unit of the product:

Material	1 kilo at £8 per kilo
Labour	30 minutes at £14 per hour
Production time	20 minutes

Complete the table below (to two decimal places) to calculate the total unit cost, using the three overhead absorption rates you have calculated in task 1.

Cost	Machine hour (£)	Labour hour (£)	Unit (£)
Material			
Labour			
Direct cost			
Overheads			
Total unit cost			

MANUFACTURING ACCOUNTS

64   JOKER LTD

Reorder the following costs into a manufacturing account format on the right side of the table below for the year ended 31 December.

	£		£
Closing inventory of work in progress	52,000		
Direct labour	140,000		
Opening inventory of raw materials	50,000		
Closing inventory of finished goods	61,000		
Closing inventory of raw materials	65,000		
Manufacturing overheads	85,000		
COST OF GOODS SOLD			
MANUFACTURING COST			
Purchases of raw materials	120,000		
Opening inventory of work in progress	48,000		
Opening inventory of finished goods	57,000		
DIRECT COST			
DIRECT MATERIALS USED			
COST OF GOODS MANUFACTURED			

Enter the correct figures for the following costs which were not provided in the table above.

	£
DIRECT MATERIALS USED	
DIRECT COST	
MANUFACTURING COST	
COST OF GOODS MANUFACTURED	
COST OF GOODS SOLD	

65 TUT LTD

Reorder the following costs into a manufacturing account format on the right side of the table below for the year ended 31 July.

	£		£
COST OF GOODS MANUFACTURED			
Opening inventory of work in progress	12,000		
Opening inventory of raw materials	10,000		
COST OF GOODS SOLD			
Closing inventory of finished goods	20,000		
Closing inventory of raw materials	12,000		
Manufacturing overheads	45,000		
MANUFACTURING COST			
Purchases of raw materials	60,000		
Opening inventory of finished goods	18,000		
DIRECT COST			
Direct labour	88,000		
Closing inventory of work in progress	15,000		
DIRECT MATERIALS USED			

Enter the correct figures for the following costs which were not provided in the table above.

	£
DIRECT MATERIALS USED	
DIRECT COST	
MANUFACTURING COST	
COST OF GOODS MANUFACTURED	
COST OF GOODS SOLD	

66   RIDDLER LTD

Riddler Ltd has the following cost information for its last quarter:

	£
Materials costs:	
Materials forming part of the product	100,000
Materials not forming part of the product	25,000
Labour costs:	
Labour working on production	194,000
Labour supporting work on production	12,000
Factory indirect expenses	75,000

Relevant inventory changes were as follows:

	£
Raw materials:	
Opening	20,000
Closing	22,000
Work in progress:	
Opening	31,000
Closing	35,000
Finished goods:	
Opening	60,000
Closing	50,000

Complete the table below to show Riddler's cost structure for the last quarter:

	£
Prime cost	
Manufacturing overhead	
Total manufacturing cost	
Cost of goods manufactured	
Cost of goods sold	

67   CLOCKING LTD

Clocking Ltd has the following information for its last quarter:

	£
Materials costs:	
Direct	50,000
Indirect	8,000
Labour costs:	
Direct	97,000
Indirect	10,000
Manufacturing expenses	53,000

Relevant inventory changes were as follows:

	£
Raw materials:	
Opening	7,000
Closing	10,000
Work in progress:	
Opening	8,000
Closing	10,000
Finished goods:	
Opening	30,000
Closing	25,000

Complete the table below to show Clocking Ltd's cost structure for the last quarter:

	£
Prime cost	
Manufacturing overhead	
Total manufacturing cost	
Cost of goods manufactured	
Cost of goods sold	

68   BOOKWORM LTD

Reorder the following costs into a manufacturing account format on the right side of the table below for the year ended 31 December. Enter the correct figures for the costs in bold that are not provided.

	£		£
DIRECT COST			
Direct labour	15,000		
MANUFACTURING COST			
Opening inventory of raw materials	5,000		
Closing inventory of finished goods	16,000		
Purchases of raw materials	15,000		
DIRECT MATERIALS USED			
Manufacturing overheads	25,000		
Closing inventory of raw materials	8,000		
COST OF GOODS SOLD			
COST OF GOODS MANUFACTURED			
Opening inventory of finished goods	12,000		
Opening inventory of work in progress	4,000		
Closing inventory of work in progress	6,000		

69   MULTI

Within a manufacturing account, the manufacturing costs are £45,000. Opening work in progress is £11,000, while opening finished goods were costed at £8,100. Closing work in progress is £9,700, while closing finished goods were £8,900.

What is Multi's cost of goods sold?

A   £44,500

B   £48,700

C   £45,500

D   £41,300

COSTING FOR INVENTORY AND WORK-IN-PROGRESS

NARRATIVE STYLE QUESTIONS

70   BOBBLE LTD

Match the disadvantage to the method of stock valuation by placing a tick in the relevant column of the table below:

Characteristic	FIFO	LIFO	AVCO
• Potentially out of date valuation on issues.			
• The valuation of inventory rarely reflects the actual purchase price of the material.			
• Potentially out of date closing inventory valuation.			

71   LINT LTD

Identify the following statements as either true or false by putting a tick in the relevant column of the table below:

Statement	True	False
• In periods of rising prices, FIFO gives a higher valuation of closing inventory than LIFO or AVCO.		
• In periods of falling prices, LIFO gives a higher valuation of issues of inventory than FIFO or AVCO.		
• AVCO would normally be expected to produce a valuation of closing inventory somewhere between valuations under FIFO and LIFO.		

72   FLUFF LTD

Identify the correct inventory valuation method from the characteristic given by putting a tick in the relevant column of the table below:

Characteristic	FIFO	LIFO	AVCO
• This inventory valuation method is particularly suited to inventory that consist of liquid materials e.g. oil.			
• This inventory valuation method is particularly suited to inventory that has a short shelf life e.g. dairy products.			
• This inventory valuation method is suited to a wheat farmer who has large silos of grain. Grain is added to and taken from the top of these silos.			

73 FIDO LTD

Identify the correct inventory valuation method from the characteristic given by putting a tick in the relevant column of the table below:

Characteristic	FIFO	LIFO	AVCO
• In times of rising prices this method will give higher profits.			
• In times of rising prices this method will give lower profits.			
• In times of rising prices this method gives a middle level of profits compared to the other two.			

74 TRUFFEAUX LTD

Identify whether the following statements are true or false by putting a tick in the relevant column of the table below:

Statement	True	False
• FIFO costs issues of inventory at the most recent purchase price.		
• AVCO costs issues of inventory at the oldest purchase price.		
• LIFO costs issues of inventory at the oldest purchase price.		
• FIFO values closing inventory at the most recent purchase price.		
• LIFO values closing inventory at the most recent purchase price.		
• AVCO values closing inventory at the latest purchase price.		

75 STOCKY LTD

Identify the correct inventory valuation method from the characteristic given by putting a tick in the relevant column of the table below:

Characteristic	FIFO	LIFO	AVCO
• Issues are valued at the most recent purchase cost.			
• Inventory is valued at the average of the cost of purchases.			
• Inventory is valued at the most recent purchase cost.			

IDENTIFICATION OF INVENTORY VALUATION METHOD

76 EPIC LTD

You are told that the opening inventory of a single raw material in the stores is 8,000 units at £5 per unit. During the month, 12,000 units at £4.50 were received and the following week 14,000 units were issued.

Task 1

Identify the valuation method described in the statements below:

Characteristic		FIFO	LIFO	AVCO
•	Closing inventory is valued at £28,200.			
•	The issue of inventory is valued at £67,000.			
•	The issue of inventory is valued at £64,000.			

Task 2

Identify whether the statements in the table below are true or false by putting a tick in the relevant column.

		True	False
•	AVCO values the issue of inventory at £65,800.		
•	LIFO values the closing inventory at £27,000.		
•	FIFO values the closing inventory at £30,000.		

77 AWESOME LTD

You are told that the opening inventory of a single raw material in the stores is 6,000 units at £6 per unit. During the month, another 6,000 units at £10 were received and the following week 7,150 units were issued.

Task 1

Identify the valuation method described in the statements below:

Characteristic		FIFO	LIFO	AVCO
•	Closing inventory is valued at £48,500.			
•	The issue of inventory is valued at £57,200.			
•	The issue of inventory is valued at £66,900.			

Task 2

Identify whether the statements in the table below are true or false by putting a tick in the relevant column.

		True	False
•	FIFO values the issue of inventory at £47,500.		
•	AVCO values the closing inventory at £38,400.		
•	LIFO values the closing inventory at £29,100.		

78   AMAZING LTD

You are told that the opening inventory of a single raw material in the stores is 2,000 units at £1.50 per unit. During the month, another 5,000 units at £5 were received and the following week 6,000 units were issued.

Task 1

Identify the valuation method described in the statements below:

Characteristic	FIFO	LIFO	AVCO
• Closing inventory is valued at £1,500.			
• The issue of inventory is valued at £23,000.			
• The issue of inventory is valued at £24,000.			

Task 2

Identify whether the statements in the table below are true or false by putting a tick in the relevant column.

	True	False
• LIFO values the issue of inventory at £26,500.		
• AVCO values the closing inventory at £5,000.		
• LIFO values the closing inventory at £4,000.		

INVENTORY CARDS

79   STONE LTD

Stone Ltd sells stone to builders. It had the following movements in one type of stone for the month of June.

DATE	RECEIPTS		ISSUES	
	Tonnes	Cost	Tonnes	Cost
June 1	500	£7,500		
June 8	350	£6,125		
June 15	275	£4,950		
June 22			650	
June 29	500	£8,750		

Complete the table below for the issue and closing inventory values, stating your answers to the nearest pound.

Method	Cost of issue on 22 June	Closing inventory at 30 June
FIFO	£	£
LIFO	£	£
AVCO	£	£

80   NATAL LTD

Natal Ltd makes and sells a wide range of clothes for babies. The following is an inventory card for Natal's most popular product for the month of December.

DATE	RECEIPTS		ISSUES	
	Units	Cost	Units	Cost
December 3	10,000	£85,000		
December 18	14,000	£112,000		
December 19	50,000	£350,000		
December 25			72,500	
December 29	5,000	£30,000		

Task 1

Complete the table below for the issue and closing inventory values. Give your answers to the nearest pound.

Method	Cost of issue on 25 Dec	Closing inventory at 29 Dec
LIFO	£	£
AVCO	£	£

Task 2

Identify the following statements as true or false by putting a tick in the relevant column of the table below:

	True	False
• FIFO would give a lower closing inventory valuation on the 29 December than LIFO and AVCO.		
• FIFO would give a lower cost of issue on the 25 December than LIFO and AVCO.		

81   GANDALF LTD

Gandalf Ltd has the following movements in a certain type of inventory into and out of its stores for the month of July.

DATE	RECEIPTS			ISSUES			BALANCE
	Units	Unit cost	Total £	Units	Unit cost	Total £	Total £
July 2	600	£1.50	£900				
July 4	500	£1.70	£850				
July 15				620			
July 19	200	£1.80	£360				
July 31				400			

Calculate the costs of the issues made on July 15 and July 31 if Gandalf plc uses a LIFO inventory valuation method.

	Valuation £
• July 15	
• July 31	

82   GRUNDY LTD

Grundy Ltd has the following movements in a certain type of inventory into and out of its stores for the month of October.

DATE	RECEIPTS		ISSUES	
	Units	Cost	Units	Cost
October 9	6000	£15,000		
October 12	3000	£6,000		
October 20	3000	£3,000		
October 25			8500	
October 30	1000	£1,500		

Complete the table below for the issue and closing inventory values.

Method	Cost of issue on 25 October	Closing inventory at 31 October
FIFO	£	£
LIFO	£	£
AVCO	£	£

83   LOBO LTD

Lobo Ltd has the following movements in a certain type of inventory into and out of its stores for the month of May.

DATE	RECEIPTS		ISSUES	
	Units	Cost	Units	Cost
May 12	250	£1,375		
May 17	400	£1,800		
May 18	600	£1,200		
May 29			500	
May 30	100	£375		

Complete the table below for the issue and closing inventory values.

Method	Cost of issue on 29 May	Closing inventory at 30 May
FIFO	£	£
LIFO	£	£
AVCO	£	£

84   ZOD LTD

Zod Ltd has the following movements in a certain type of inventory into and out of it stores for the month of February.

DATE	RECEIPTS		ISSUES	
	Units	Cost	Units	Cost
February 2	100	£500		
February 3			50	
February 12	150	£600		
February 16			60	
February 20	110	£505		
February 26			40	

Complete the table below for the issue and closing inventory values. State your answer to the nearest pound.

Method	Cost of issue on 16 February	Closing inventory at 26 February
FIFO	£	£
AVCO	£	£

COSTING FOR LABOUR

NARRATIVE STYLE QUESTIONS

85   NULAB LTD

Identify the labour payment method by putting a tick in the relevant column of the table below:

Payment method	Time-rate	Piecework	Piece-rate plus bonus
• Labour is paid based solely on the production achieved.			
• Labour is paid extra if an agreed level of output is exceeded.			
• Labour is paid according to hours worked.			

86   LU LTD

Identify one advantage for each labour payment method by putting a tick in the relevant column of the table below:

Payment method	Time-rate	Piecework	Time-rate plus bonus
• Assured level of remuneration for employee.			
• Employee earns more if they work more efficiently than expected.			
• Assured level of remuneration and reward for working efficiently.			

87   MANDELA LTD

Identify whether the following statements are true or false in the relevant column of the table below:

Statement	True	False
• Time rate is paid based on the production achieved.		
• Overtime is paid for hours worked over the standard hours agreed.		
• Piece rate is paid according to hours worked.		

88   PERRES LTD

Identify the hourly payment method by putting a tick in the relevant column of the table below:

Payment method	Basic rate	Overtime premium	Overtime rate
• This is the amount paid above the basic rate for hours worked in excess of the normal hours.			
• This is the total amount paid per hour for hours worked in excess of the normal hours.			
• This is the amount paid per hour for normal hours worked.			

89   TEVEZ LTD

Identify the following statements as true or false by putting a tick in the relevant column of the table below:

Statement	True	False
• Direct labour costs can be identified with the goods being made or the service being provided.		
• Indirect labour costs vary directly with the level of activity.		

90   BERDYCH LTD

Identify the whether the labour payment is usually associated with a fixed or variable cost by putting a tick in the relevant column of the table below:

Payment method	Variable	Fixed
• Labour that is paid based on a time rate basis per hour worked.		
• Labour is paid on a monthly salary basis.		
• Labour that is based on number of units produced.		

91   SODERLING LTD

Identify each labour payment method by putting a tick in the relevant column of the table below:

Payment method	Time-rate	Piecework	Salary
• Assured level of remuneration for employee usually agreed for the year.			
• Employee earnings are directly linked with units they produce.			
• Employee earnings are directly linked with hours they work.			

92   MURRAY LTD

Identify the following statements as true or false by putting a tick in the relevant column of the table below:

	True	False
• Indirect labour costs includes production supervisors' salaries.		
• Direct labour costs usually vary directly with the level of activity.		

93   OWEN LTD

Identify one advantage for each labour payment method by putting a tick in the relevant column of the table below:

Payment method	Time-rate	Piecework	Salary
• Employee is paid the same amount every month.			
• Employee wage increases in direct correlation with the number of hours worked.			
• Employee wage increases in direct correlation with the number of units produced.			

94 PIECEWORK STATEMENTS

Identify the following statements as either true or false by putting a tick in the relevant column of the table below:

Statement	True	False
• Piecework encourages employees to work harder.		
• Piecework requires accurate recording of the number of hours staff have worked.		
• Piecework encourages workers to improve the quality of the units they produce.		

CALCULATING LABOUR COSTS

95 MUTANT LTD

Mutant Ltd pays a time-rate of £7.50 per hour to its direct labour for a standard 32 hour week. Any of the labour force working in excess of 32 hours is paid an overtime rate of time and a half.

Calculate the following figures for the week for the two workers in the table below, entering your answers to the nearest pound.

Worker	Hours worked	Basic wage	Overtime	Gross wage
S. Torm	34 hours	£	£	£
J. Grey	38 hours	£	£	£

96 PHOENIX LTD

Phoenix plc pays its employees £8.00 per hour and expects them to make 20 units per hour. Any excess production will be paid a bonus of £1.50 per unit.

Identify the following statements as being true or false by putting a tick in the relevant column of the table below:

Statement	True	False
An employee who works 38 hours and makes 775 units will not receive a bonus.		
An employee who works 40 hours and makes 815 units will receive total pay of £342.50.		
An employee who works 37 hours and makes 744 units will earn a bonus of £6.		

97 KAHN LTD

Kahn Ltd uses a time-rate method with bonus to pay its direct labour in one of its factories. The time-rate used is £12 per hour and a worker is expected to produce 5 units an hour, any time saved is paid at £6 per hour.

Calculate the gross wage for the week including bonus for the three workers in the table below:

Worker	Hours worked	Units produced	Basic wage	Bonus	Gross wage
A. Smith	35	175	£	£	£
J. O'Hara	35	180	£	£	£
M.Stizgt	35	185	£	£	£

98 ENTERPRISE LTD

Enterprise Ltd has a production target for its employees of 400 units per week. Employees are rewarded with a bonus for excess production, at a rate of £6 per unit, capped at a maximum of 450 units.

Identify whether the bonus calculations for the following employees are correct:

Bonus calculation	Correct	Incorrect
Javier produced 400 units and earned a bonus of £6.		
Esha produced 465 units and earned a bonus of £390.		
Mika produced 480 units and earned a bonus of £300.		

99 SGC LTD

SGC Ltd uses a basic salary plus piecework method to pay labour in one of its factories. The basic salary is £285 per week the piece rate used is £0.75 per unit produced.

Calculate the gross wage for the week for the two workers in the table below. Enter your answer to the nearest penny.

Worker	Units produced in week	Gross wage
J. O'Neill	500 units	£
S. Carter	650 units	£

100 GOTHIC LTD

Gothic Ltd employs 5 production workers in its factory. All production workers are paid a basic rate of £17 per hour.

The factory sets a total production target for output each week, at 20,000 units. A bonus of £30 per worker is paid for each complete percent that actual output exceeds the target.

Last week, the actual output was 22,100 units.

Identify whether the following statements about the labour cost for Gothic Ltd are correct or incorrect for the following employees:

Pay calculation	Correct	Incorrect
M. Shelley worked for 35 hours and earned total income of £595.		
G. Leroux worked for 37 hours and earned total income of £929.		
A.E. Poe worked for 32 hours and earned total income of £874.		
The total bonus paid by Gothic Ltd was £1,500.		

101 AVENGERS LTD

Avengers Ltd pays a time-rate of £10 per hour to its direct labour force a standard 35 hour week. Any of the labour force working in excess of this over the four week period is paid an overtime rate of time and a quarter.

Calculate the gross wage for the **4-week** period for the three workers in the table below. Enter your answers to the nearest pound.

Worker	Hours worked	Basic wage	Overtime	Gross wage
T. Stark	138	£	£	£
B. Banner	142	£	£	£
S. Rogers	145	£	£	£

102 DRACO LTD

Draco Ltd uses a piecework method to pay labour in one of its factories. The rate used is 80p per unit produced up to the standard number of units to be produced per week of 250. For any units over that the workers will get £10 per 20 units.

Calculate the gross wage for the week for the three workers in the table below:

Worker	Units produced in week	Gross wage
P. Jones	240 units	£
D. Bannatyne	350 units	£
L. Redford	250 units	£

103 QUAGGA PLC

Quagga plc pays its employees £4.50 per hour and expects them to make 50 units per hour. Any excess production will be paid a bonus of 45p per unit.

Identify the following statements as being true or false by putting a tick in the relevant column of the table below:

Statement	True	False
During a 29 hour week, an employee producing 1,475 units would not receive a bonus.		
During a 32 hour week, an employee producing 1,665 units would receive a bonus of £29.25.		
During a 37 hour week, an employee producing 1,925 units would receive total pay of £300.25.		

104 JLA PLC

JLA plc pays its employees £5 per hour and expects them to make 6 units per hour. Any time saved will be paid as a bonus at £8 per hour.

Identify the following statements as being true or false by putting a tick in the relevant column of the table below:

Statement	True	False
During a 30 hour week, an employee producing 192 units would receive a bonus of £16.		
During a 35 hour week, an employee producing 240 units would receive total pay of £215.		
During a 30 hour week, an employee producing 180 units would not receive a bonus.		

105 INJUSTICE LTD

Davidson Ltd pays a basic wage of £175/week plus £1.20 per unit produced.

Calculate the gross wage for the week for the three workers in the table below:

Worker	Units produced	Basic wage	Piece work	Gross wage
N. Wing	295	£	£	£
W. Woman	355	£	£	£
T. Flash	385	£	£	£

106 GREENWOOD LTD

Greenwood Ltd pays a basic wage of £350/week equivalent to a time-rate of £10 per hour and a standard 35 hour week. Workers are expected to produce 5 units an hour and for units produced in excess of this a bonus is paid based on £7 for every hour saved.

So, for example, if 10 additional units are produced, then this would be equivalent to two hours saved and a bonus of £14 awarded.

Calculate the gross wage for the week including bonus for the three workers in the table below:

Worker	Hours worked	Units produced	Basic wage	Bonus	Gross wage
B. Ryan	35	175	£	£	£
S. Chang	35	190	£	£	£
E. Schneider	35	210	£	£	£

VARIANCES

NARRATIVE QUESTIONS

107 VARIOUS LTD

Identify the following statements as being true or false by putting a tick in the relevant column of the table below:

Statement	True	False
• A variance is the difference between budgeted and actual cost.		
• A favourable variance could arise due to actual costs being less than budgeted.		
• An adverse variance could arise due to actual income being less than budgeted.		
• A favourable variance occurs when actual income is the same as budgeted income.		

108 JONES LTD

Identify the following statements as being true or false by putting a tick in the relevant column of the table below:

Statement	True	False
If budgeted sales are 6,000 units at £7.50 per unit and actual sales are £47,600, the sales variance is favourable		
A favourable cost variance occurs when an actual cost of £9,800 is compared to a budgeted cost of £24 per unit for a budgeted output of 400 units		
A variance arises from a comparison of budgeted costs for last year with actual costs for this year		
If actual material costs are the same as budgeted costs for materials then no variance arises		

109 GATLAND LTD

Identify the following statements as being true or false by putting a tick in the relevant column of the table below:

Statement	True	False
If budgeted sales are 4,000 units at £9.50 per unit and actual sales are £35,200, the sales variance is favourable		
A favourable cost variance occurs when an actual cost of £6,400 is compared to a budgeted cost of £14 per unit for a budgeted output of 500 units		
A variance arises from a comparison of budgeted costs for last year with budgeted costs for this year		
If actual material costs are the same as budgeted costs for materials then the materials variance is adverse		

110 LANCASTER LTD

Identify the following statements as being true or false by putting a tick in the relevant column of the table below:

Statement	True	False
If budgeted sales are 14,000 units at £3.50 per unit and actual sales are £45,200, the sales variance is favourable		
An adverse cost variance occurs when an actual cost of £68,400 is compared to a budgeted cost of £14 per unit for a budgeted output of 5,000 units		
A variance arises from a comparison of budgeted costs for this year with actual costs for this year		
If actual material costs are the same as budgeted costs for materials then the materials variance is favourable		

111 GOODE LTD

Identify the following statements as being true or false by putting a tick in the relevant column of the table below:

Statement	True	False
The variance for the Direct Material cost of Department B should be reported to the purchasing manager		
The variance for the Direct Labour cost for Department A should be reported to the sales manager		
The variance for the Direct Labour cost for Department B should be reported to the production manager of Department A		
A Direct Material cost variance that has been deemed Not Significant should not be reported		

112 BROWN LTD

Identify the following statements as being true or false by putting a tick in the relevant column of the table below:

Statement	True	False
The variance for the Direct Material cost of Department A should be reported to the purchasing manager		
The variance for the Direct Labour cost for Department A should be reported to the production manager of Department B		
The variance for sales should be reported to the sales manager		
A Direct Material cost variance that has been deemed Significant should not be reported		

VARIANCE CALCULATION QUESTIONS

113 EREBOR PLC

Erebor Ltd has produced a performance report detailing budgeted and actual cost for last month.

Calculate the amount of the variance for each cost type and then determine whether it is adverse or favourable (enter A or F).

Cost type	Budget £	Actual £	Variance £	Adverse or favourable (A or F)
Sales	600,500	597,800		
Direct materials	205,800	208,500		
Direct labour	155,000	154,800		
Production overheads	65,000	72,100		
Administration overheads	58,400	55,200		

114 MORIA LTD

The following performance report for this month has been produced for Moria Ltd. Any variance in excess of 7% of budget is deemed to be significant.

Calculate the variance as a % of the budget and enter your answer into the table below to the **nearest whole percentage**. Indicate whether the variance is significant or not by entering S for significant and NS for not significant.

Cost type	Budget	Variance	Variance as % of budget	Significant or Not significant
Sales	45,100	4,214		
Material	15,750	1,260		
Labour	12,915	805		
Variable overheads	5,750	315		
Fixed overheads	8,155	1,011		

115 WYEDALE LTD

Wyedale Ltd has produced a performance report detailing budgeted and actual cost for last month.

Calculate the amount of the variance in £ and % for each cost type and then determine whether it is adverse or favourable by putting an A or F in the relevant column of the table below. State your percentage to the nearest whole number.

Cost type	Budget £	Actual £	Variance £	Variance %	Adverse/ Favourable
Sales	27,000	29,775			
Direct materials	7,400	8,510			
Direct labour	7,200	7,920			
Production overheads	5,500	5,390			
Administration overheads	4,500	4,365			

116   BELEGOST LTD

The following performance report for this month has been produced for Belegost Ltd as summarised in the table below. Any variance in excess of 6% of budget is deemed to be significant and should be reported to the relevant manager for review and appropriate action.

Determine whether the variance for each figure is adverse or favourable by putting an A or F into the relevant column of the table below. Put an S in the relevant column if the variance is significant or an NS if the variance is not significant.

	Budget £	Actual £	Adverse or Favourable (A or F)	Significant or not significant (S or NS)
Sales	205,000	207,100		
Direct materials	75,150	78,750		
Direct labour	110,556	107,950		
Production overheads	14,190	12,500		
Non-production overheads	16,190	17,880		

117   IVAN LTD

Ivan Ltd has produced a performance report detailing budgeted and actual cost for last month.

Calculate the amount of the variance for each cost type and then determine whether it is adverse or favourable by putting an A or an F into the relevant column below:

Cost type	Budget £	Actual £	Variance £	Adverse or Favourable (A or F)
Sales	544,750	547,450		
Direct materials	76,800	80,200		
Direct labour	148,400	146,000		
Production overheads	136,000	144,200		
Administration overheads	105,000	109,800		

118 BLUEBELL LTD

The following performance report for this month has been produced for Bluebell Ltd as summarised in the table below.

Calculate the variances in the table below and indicate whether they are adverse or favourable by putting an A or F in the relevant column and calculate the variance as a % to the nearest whole number.

Cost type	Budget £	Actual £	Variance £	Adverse/ Favourable	%
Sales	£204,555	£197,455			
Direct materials	£39,000	£42,300			
Direct labour	£75,000	£83,000			
Production overheads	£69,000	£64,800			
Administration overheads	£53,000	£58,900			

119 TELMAH LTD

You have been provided with the following information about performance in the previous month.

Cost type	Budget £	Actual £	Variance £	Variance %	Significant/ not significant	Report to
Sales	310,000	353,400				
Fuel costs	25,000	31,250				
Entertaining	16,000	15,500				

Reporting policies state that:

- Variances in excess of 5% of budget and that are greater than £500 are significant. They should be reported to the department manager (DM).

- Adverse variances in excess of 10% of budget, and that are greater than £1,000 are significant. They should be reported to the department director (DD).

- Variances in excess of 20% of budget, and that are greater than £1,500 are significant. They should be reported to the department director (DD).

Complete the table above to show each variance and variance percentage. Identify whether each variance is significant or not and who (if anyone) the variance should be reported to.

Section 2

ANSWERS TO PRACTICE QUESTIONS

COST CLASSIFICATION

FINANCIAL AND MANAGEMENT ACCOUNTING

1   FAMA

Characteristic	Financial accounting	Management accounting
• Have to be produced annually.	✓	
• Analyses historic events to help produce forecasts.		✓
• Is always produced using accounting standards.	✓	
• Is produced on an ad hoc basis when required.		✓

2   FINANCIAL AND MANAGEMENT

Characteristic	Financial accounting	Management accounting
• Must be presented as specified by the Companies Act and accounting standards.	✓	
• Helps managers run the business on a day-to-day basis.		✓
• Used as the basis for the calculation of the organisation's tax charge.	✓	
• Can include anything that managers feel is useful for the business.		✓

3 MAFA

Characteristic	Management accounting	Financial accounting
• It is based on past events.		✓
• Its purpose is to provide information for managers.	✓	
• It is based on future events.	✓	
• It complies with company law and accounting rules.		✓

4 FEATURES

Feature	Financial accounting	Management accounting
• Analysis of profit by cost centre.		✓
• Statement of profit or loss using format as dictated by accounting standards and company law.	✓	
• Cash flow forecasts.		✓
• Cost per unit calculation.		✓

COST AND PROFIT CENTRES

5 JEREMY

	Cost centre	Profit centre
• Bakery	✓	
• Shop		✓
• Office	✓	

6 PRINT PLC

Department	Cost centre	Profit centre
• Binding		✓
• Shops		✓
• Marketing	✓	

7   HOOCH PLC

Department	Cost centre	Profit centre	Investment centre
• Hooch's manager has no responsibility for income or asset purchases and disposals.	✓		
• Hooch's manager is assessed on the profitability of their department, as well as how effectively they have controlled their assets.			✓
• Hooch's manager is responsible for income and expenditure of their department only.		✓	

CLASSIFYING COSTS BY ELEMENT (MATERIALS, LABOUR OR OVERHEADS)

8   VVV LTD

Cost	Materials	Labour	Overheads
• Paint used on the planes.	✓		
• Depreciation of the machines used in the factory.			✓
• Oil used on the machines in the factory.			✓
• Salary of worker assembling the planes.		✓	

9   TRIP LTD

Cost	Materials	Labour	Overheads
• Wages of the insurance clerks dealing with claims.		✓	
• Rent of the office.			✓
• Paper used to print off insurance policies.	✓		
• Salary of the office manager.		✓	

10   FRUWT LTD

Cost	Materials	Labour	Overheads
• Purchase of fruit for juicing.	✓		
• Electricity used by juicing machines.			✓
• Water added to the juice before sale.	✓		
• Wages of staff operating juicing machinery.		✓	

11   MARTINA

Cost	Materials	Labour	Overheads
• Stationery used in Martina's court cases.	✓		
• Wages of Martina's secretary.		✓	
• Water rates for Martina's office.			✓
• Cost of training courses taken by Martina.			✓

CLASSIFYING COSTS BY NATURE (DIRECT OR INDIRECT)

12   KHALED

Cost	Direct	Indirect
• Paper used in the newspapers.	✓	
• Wages of warehouse staff.		✓
• Heat and light for head office.		✓
• Ink used in printing the newspapers.	✓	

13   RUSSETT LTD

Cost	Direct	Indirect
• Glass used to make tablets.	✓	
• Insurance of factory.		✓
• Wages of workers assembling tablets.	✓	
• Cost of entertaining corporate clients.		✓

14   SCOTLAND LTD

Cost	Direct	Indirect
• Cleaners' wages.		✓
• Advertising expense.		✓
• Material used in production.	✓	
• Production manager's wages.		✓
• Machinist wages.	✓	

15   DIRECT OR INDIRECT

Cost	Direct	Indirect
• Chargeable hour for a lawyer.	✓	
• Machine hire for a building contractor in a long term contract.	✓	
• Electricity for a garden centre.		✓
• Audit fee for a restaurant.		✓

16 DIRECT COSTS

B

Direct costs are variable and are therefore usually assumed to be constant, regardless of the level of activity within the relevant range. Answer A is incorrect because it describes the behaviour of a fixed cost within the relevant range of activity. Answer C also describes a fixed cost, since the same total fixed cost would be shared over a varying number of units, resulting in a unit cost that varies with changes in activity levels. Answer D is incorrect because total variable costs are conventionally deemed to remain unaltered when activity levels remain constant.

CLASSIFYING COSTS BY FUNCTION (PRODUCTION, ADMINISTRATION OR SELLING AND DISTRIBUTION)

17 NOOGLE LTD

Cost	Production	Administration	Selling and distribution
• Purchases of plastic for ready meal containers.	✓		
• Depreciation of sales department's delivery lorries.			✓
• Insurance of office computers.		✓	
• Salaries of production workers.	✓		

18 HEAVING LTD

Cost	Production	Administration	Selling and distribution
• Paper used to print off sales invoices.		✓	
• Metal used to make weights and bars.	✓		
• Depreciation of sales person's vehicle.			✓
• Repairs to machine in factory.	✓		

19   KORMA PLC

Cost	Production	Administration	Selling and distribution	Finance
• Direct materials.	✓			
• Sales director's salary.			✓	
• Head office printer ink.		✓		
• Direct labour.	✓			
• Bank charges.				✓

20   JAMES

Cost	Production	Administration	Selling and distribution	Finance
• Salary of receptionist.		✓		
• Plastic used in false teeth.	✓			
• Stationery provided to all departments.		✓		
• Interest on James' bank overdraft.				✓
• Electricity for James' factory.	✓			

CLASSIFYING COSTS BY BEHAVIOUR (FIXED, VARIABLE OR SEMI-VARIABLE)

21   QUARK LTD

Cost	Fixed	Variable	Semi-variable
• Bar manager's salary.	✓		
• Alcohol used to make drinks.		✓	
• Rent of bar.	✓		
• Telephone costs, including standard line rental charge.			✓

22   MORN LTD

Cost	Fixed	Variable	Semi-variable
• Wood used in production.		✓	
• Advertising manager's salary.	✓		
• Electricity costs which include a standing charge.			✓
• Labour costs paid on a piecework basis.		✓	

23 STEPPED FIXED COST

A

A supervisor's wages are usually classified as a step cost because a supervisor may be responsible for supervising up to a specific number of workers. However, if output increases such that additional direct labour is required, then an extra supervisor will be required.

1 – 10 workers	1 supervisor
11 – 20 workers	2 supervisors

24 BRAETAK LTD

Cost	Fixed	Variable	Semi-variable
• Rent of an office building.	✓		
• Wages of production staff paid on an hourly basis.		✓	
• Wages of production staff paid by a piece rate method.		✓	
• Sales staff paid a basic wage plus commission for each unit sold.			✓

Note: the piece rate scheme does not mention a guaranteed minimum wage so the correct answer is variable.

25 ODO LTD

Cost	Fixed	Variable	Semi-variable
• Material used in the production process.		✓	
• Safety review fee for the year.	✓		
• Electricity costs which include a standing charge.			✓
• Labour paid on a per unit basis.		✓	

26 DEFINITIONS

Behaviour	Fixed	Variable	Semi-variable	Stepped cost
• This type of cost increases in direct proportion to the amount of units produced.		✓		
• This type of cost has a fixed and a variable element.			✓	
• This type of cost remains constant despite changes in output.	✓			
• This type of cost is fixed within a certain range of output.				✓

27 MATCH A GRAPH

(a) Variable cost per unit – graph 1

(b) Total fixed cost – graph 1

(c) Stepped fixed costs – graph 3

(d) Total variable cost – graph 2

(e) Semi-variable cost – graph 4

COST CODING

28 BYTES LTD

Cost	Code
• Salary of trainee IT consultant.	• B100
• Planning costs to renew lease of the office.	• C200
• Wages of the office manager.	• B200
• Cleaning materials used by cleaner.	• A200

29 HERO LTD

Transaction	Code
• Cost of major advertising campaign.	• 760/340
• Oil for machine in factory.	• 225/115
• Silk used in manufacturing of costumes.	• 225/110
• Insurance of head office.	• 485/230
• Sale of women's costumes to a supermarket chain.	• 115/085
• Wages paid to delivery van drivers.	• 760/340

30 VILLAIN LTD

Transaction	Code
• Petrol used to run drilling machinery.	• 015/200
• Sale of silver to a jewellery manufacturer.	• 011/200
• Replacement of worn out drilling machinery parts.	• 015/200
• Depreciation of fleet of delivery lorries.	• 024/200
• Salary of finance director.	• 019/200
• Sale of gold to an electronics company.	• 011/100

31 NAYULZ LTD

Cost	Code
• Income earned from salons in New York City, America.	RE228
• Bank loans raised to open a new store in London.	IN100
• Nail polish purchased for use in salon.	CO315
• Heat and light for salon.	CO325
• Nayulz funds invested in new project.	IN110

32 JUMPER LTD

Sale	Code
• Sale of one jumper to Mrs S. Wooley.	KNI/315
• Sale of protective trousers to a factory in London.	TRS/635
• Sale of large coats to an office in Birmingham.	MCN/515
• Sale of woolen jumpers to a shop in Halifax.	KNI/425
• Sale of four coats to Mr A. West.	MCN/315
• Sale of three hundred trousers to a shop in Manchester.	TRS/425

33 GREENFINGERS

Cost	Code
• Purchase of seeds used to grow plants for resale.	CS880
• External loans for investment in new greenhouses.	IN515
• Wages of gardeners who maintain the plants to be sold.	CS890
• Sales of food and drink.	RV795

COST BEHAVIOUR

CALCULATION QUESTIONS

34 HULK PLC

Statement	Fixed	Variable	Semi-variable
• Costs are £37,500 when 7,500 units are made and £62,500 when 12,500 units are made.		✓	
• Costs are £2 per unit when 7,500 units are made and £1.20 per unit when 12,500 units are made.	✓		
• Costs are £50,000 when 7,500 units are made and £80,000 when 12,500 units are made.			✓

35 BANNER PLC

Statement	Fixed	Variable	Semi-variable
• Costs are £5,000 plus £45 per unit, regardless of the number of units made.			✓
• Costs are £5,000 when 300 units are made and £5,000 when 600 units are made.	✓		
• Costs are £35 per unit regardless of the number of units made.		✓	

36 NORTON PLC

Statement	Fixed	Variable	Semi-variable
• Costs are £50,000 in total regardless of the number of units made.	✓		
• Costs are £50,000 in total when 2,500 units are made and £80,000 when 4,000 units are made.		✓	
• Costs are £7 per unit when 1,000 units are made and £6 per unit when 2,000 units are made.			✓

Note: The third cost must be semi-variable as it cannot be fixed (it changes as the number of units changes) and it cannot be purely variable as the cost per unit changes at different levels of activity.

37 TRIUMPH LTD

Task 1

Statement	Fixed	Variable	Semi-variable
At 9,000 units this cost is £29,250, and at 12,000 units it is £39,000		✓	
At 5,000 units this cost is £5.20 per unit, and at 8,000 units it is £3.25 per unit	✓		
At 19,800 units, this cost is £64,500, and at 27,000 units it is £82,500			✓

£29,250 ÷ 9,000 units = £3.25, £39,000 ÷ 12,000 units = £3.25, therefore variable cost

5,000 units × £5.20 = £26,000, 8,000 units × £3.25 = £26,000, therefore fixed cost

£64,500 ÷ 19,800 units = £3.26, £82,500 ÷ 27,000 units = £3.06, therefore must be a **semi-variable** cost – it cannot be fixed (it changes as the number of units changes) and it cannot be purely variable as the cost per unit changes at different levels of activity.

Task 2

	6,000 units	7,000 units	10,000 units	14,000 units
Variable cost (£)	18,000			42,000
Fixed cost (£)	24,000			24,000
Total cost (£)	42,000	45,000	54,000	66,000

Using the hi-lo method:

For the volumes given, difference in costs = 54,000 – 45,000 = £9,000

Difference in volumes = 10,000 – 7,000 = 3,000 units

Therefore variable cost per unit = £9,000 ÷ 3,000 units = £3/unit

At 10,000 units, fixed costs = £54,000 – (10,000 × £3) = £24,000

38   YOUNGS LTD

Task 1

Statement	Fixed	Variable	Semi-variable
At 4,000 units this cost is £3.00 per unit, and at 6,000 units it is £2.00 per unit.	✓		
At 7,000 units this cost is £32,500, and at 10,000 units it is £43,000.			✓
At 11,000 units this cost is £57,750, and at 15,000 units it is £78,750.		✓	

4,000 units × £3.00 = £12,000, 6,000 units × £2.00 = £12,000, therefore **fixed** cost

£32,500 ÷ 7,000 units = £4.64, £43,000 ÷ 10,000 units = £4.30, therefore must be a **semi-variable** cost – it cannot be fixed (it changes as the number of units changes) and it cannot be purely variable as the cost per unit changes at different levels of activity.

£57,750 ÷ 11,000 units = £5.25, £78,750 ÷ 15,000 units = £5.25, therefore **variable** cost

Task 2

	8,000 units	10,000 units	13,000 units	16,000 units
Variable cost (£)	34,000			68,000
Fixed cost (£)	18,000			18,000
Total cost (£)	52,000	60,500	73,250	86,000

Using the hi-lo method:

For the volumes given, difference in costs = 73,250 − 60,500 = £12,750

Difference in volumes = 13,000 − 10,000 = 3,000 units

Therefore variable cost per unit = £12,750 ÷ 3,000 units = £4.25/unit

At 10,000 units, fixed costs = £60,500 − (10,000 × £4.25) = £18,000

39   CARE PLC

Task 1

Statement	Fixed	Variable	Semi-variable
At 8,000 units this cost is £38,000, and at 12,000 units it is £49,000			✓
At 10,500 units this cost is £39,375, and at 14,000 units it is £52,500		✓	
At 4,000 units this cost is £4.50 per unit, and at 6,000 units is £3.00 per unit	✓		

£38,000 ÷ 8,000 units = £4.75, £49,000 ÷ 12,000 units = £4.08, therefore must be a **semi-variable** cost – it cannot be fixed (it changes as the number of units changes) and it cannot be purely variable as the cost per unit changes at different levels of activity.

£39,375 ÷ 10,500 units = £3.75, £52,500 ÷ 14,000 units = £3.75, therefore **variable** cost

4,000 units × £4.50 = £18,000, 6,000 units × £3.00 = £18,000, therefore **fixed** cost

Task 2

	3,000 units	5,000 units	9,000 units	12,000 units
Variable cost (£)	5,100			20,400
Fixed cost (£)	4,500			4,500
Total cost (£)	9,600	13,000	19,800	24,900

Using the hi-lo method:

For the volumes given, difference in costs = 19,800 – 13,000 = £6,800

Difference in volumes = 9,000 – 5,000 = 4,000 units

Therefore variable cost per unit = £6,800 ÷ 4,000 units = £1.70/unit

At 9,000 units, fixed costs = £19,800 – (9,000 × £1.70) = £4,500

40   ROBSHAW LTD

Task 1

Statement	Fixed	Variable	Semi-variable
At 6,000 units this cost is £3.75 per unit, and at 9,000 units it is £2.50 per unit	✓		
At 8,500 units this cost is £36,550, and at 11,300 units it is £48,590		✓	
At 11,000 units this cost is £27,750, and at 14,000 units it is £33,000			✓

6,000 units × £3.75 = £22,500, 9,000 units × £2.50 = £22,500, therefore **fixed** cost

£36,550 ÷ 8,500 units = £4.30, £48,590 ÷ 11,300 units = £4.30, therefore **variable** cost

£27,750 ÷ 11,000 units = £2.52, £33,000 ÷ 14,000 units = £2.36, therefore must be a **semi-variable** cost – it cannot be fixed (it changes as the number of units changes) and it cannot be purely variable as the cost per unit changes at different levels of activity.

Task 2

	9,000 units	11,000 units	14,000 units	16,500 units
Variable cost (£)	29,250			53,625
Fixed cost (£)	4,500			4,500
Total cost (£)	33,750	40,250	50,000	58,125

Using the hi-lo method:

For the volumes given, difference in costs = 50,000 – 40,250 = £9,750

Difference in volumes = 14,000 – 11,000 = 3,000 units

Therefore variable cost per unit = £9,750 ÷ 3,000 units = £3.25/unit

At 11,000 units, fixed costs = £40,250 – (11,000 × £3.25) = £4,500

NARRATIVE STYLE QUESTIONS

41 BUNGLE LTD

Statement	True	False
• Total variable costs will decrease.		✓
• Total fixed costs will remain the same.	✓	
• The variable cost per unit will remain the same.	✓	
• The fixed cost per unit will increase.		✓

42 TF

Statement	True	False
• Variable costs change directly with changes in activity.	✓	
• Fixed costs change directly with changes in activity.		✓
• Stepped costs are fixed within a set range of output.	✓	

43 FIXED OR VARIABLE

Cost	Fixed	Variable
• Direct materials.		✓
• Power used in production machinery.		✓
• Training costs for new employees in production.	✓	
• Insurance for sales cars.	✓	
• Insurance machinery.	✓	
• Sales commission.		✓

44 FOV

Cost	Fixed	Variable
• Piecework wages paid to factory workers.		✓
• Salaries paid to company directors.	✓	
• Annual payment for cleaning of air conditioning units.	✓	

45 VOF

Cost	Fixed	Variable
• Annual salaries paid to factory managers.	✓	
• Hourly wages paid to factory workers.		✓
• Colour ink used to print magazines.		✓

46 STORM

Cost	Overhead?	
	Yes	No
• Labour cost of workers who assemble the product.		✓
• Insurance cost of factory where product is assembled.	✓	
• Heat and light for manufacturing machines.	✓	

47 ROGUE

Cost	Overhead?	
	Yes	No
• Labour cost of cleaning staff in a factory.	✓	
• Depreciation of delivery vans.	✓	
• Cost of materials used to build the product.		✓

48 GAMBIT

Cost	Overhead?	
	Yes	No
• Wages of staff paid on a piecework system.		✓
• Cost of factory canteen staff hourly wages.	✓	
• Direct materials.		✓

COST CARDS, TOTAL COSTS AND UNIT COSTS

49 JEEPERS LTD

Cost	Yes	No
• Materials used in production.	✓	
• Piecework labour costs.	✓	
• Salary of chief executive.		✓

Element	Unit product cost
Materials (W1)	£35
Labour (W2)	£8
Direct cost (materials + labour)	£43
Overheads (W3)	£38
Total	£81

(W1) Total material cost for 15,000 units = 37,500kilos × £14 = £525,000

Material cost per unit = £525,000/15,000 = £35

(W2) Total labour cost for 15,000 units = 7,500 hours × £16 = £120,000

Labour cost per unit = £120,000/15,000 = £8

(W3) Overhead per unit = £570,000/15,000 = £38

50 BRANIAC LTD

Element	Unit cost
Materials	£24.50
Labour	£40.25
Direct cost	£64.75
Overheads	£12.50
Total	£77.25

51 GLORIA LTD

Element	Unit cost	Total cost for 20,000 units
Variable production costs	£5.50	£110,000
Fixed production costs	£4.00	£80,000
Total production cost	£9.50	£190,000

52   BIZARRO LTD

Element	Unit cost	Total cost
Materials	£45.00	£765,000
Labour	£9.00	£153,000
Overheads	£2.50	£42,500
Total	£56.50	£960,500

53   VINNY LTD

Element	Unit cost	Total cost
Materials	£5.00 (W1)	£100,000
Labour	£8.00 (W2)	£160,000
Overheads	£5.00 (W3)	£100,000
Total	£18.00	£360,000

(W1) Total material cost for 15,000 units = £75,000. Material cost per unit = £75,000/15,000 = £5

(W2) Total labour cost for 15,000 units = £120,000. Labour cost per unit = £120,000/15,000 = £8

(W3) Total production overheads don't change with changes in activity level. The total is simply divided across the new production level = £100,000/20,000 = £5 per unit.

54   DARKSEID LTD

Element	Unit cost
Materials	£3.50 (W1)
Labour	£6.75 (W2)
Fixed overheads	£2.42 (W3)
Total	£12.67

(W1) Total material cost for 95,000 units = 47,500kg × £7 = £332,500

 Material cost per unit = £332,500/95,000 = £3.50

(W2) Total labour cost for 95,000 units = 71,250 hrs × £9 = £641,250

Labour cost per unit = £641,250/95,000 = £6.75

(W3) Fixed overheads total does not change. The revised cost per unit is £242,000/100,000 = £2.42

55   DOOMSDAY LTD

Element	Total cost for 20,000 units	Unit cost
Direct costs	£1,250,000	£62.50
Production overhead	£75,000	£3.75
Non production overhead	£185,000	£9.25
Total costs	£1,510,000	£75.50

56   OLSEN LTD

Element	Total cost	Unit cost
Materials	£960,000	£12.00
Labour	£1,360,000	£17.00
Production overheads	£80,000	£1.00
Administration overheads	£40,000	£0.50
Total	£2,440,000	£30.50

57   FLAKEWAY LTD

Element	Unit cost
Materials	£5.00
Labour	£4.00
Fixed overheads	£2.00
Total	£11.00

58   CORONATION LTD

	Total cost for 5,000 units	Unit cost
Direct costs	£32,500	£6.50
Production overhead	£40,000	£8.00
Non production overhead	£45,000	£9.00
Total costs	£117,500	£23.50

59   LUTHOR LTD

Element	Unit cost
Materials	£60.00
Labour	£22.50
Fixed overheads	£38.00
Total	£120.50

60 WILKINSON LTD

Task 1

	Machine hour	Labour hour	Unit
Overheads (£)	150,000	150,000	150,000
Activity	10,000	12,500	60,000
Absorption rate (£)	15.00	12.00	2.50

Task 2

Cost	Machine hour (£)	Labour hour (£)	Unit (£)
Material	10.00	10.00	10.00
Labour	2.50	2.50	2.50
Direct cost	12.50	12.50	12.50
Overheads	2.50 (W1)	3.00 (W2)	2.50 (W3)
Total unit cost	15.00	15.50	15.00

(W1) Each unit requires 10 minutes of production time (or 10/60 hour). The OAR for machine time is £15.00 per hour. Therefore the overhead absorbed will be 10/60 × £15.00 = £2.50.

(W2) Each unit requires 15 minutes of labour time (or 15/60 hour). The OAR for labour time is £12.00 per hour. Therefore the overhead absorbed will be 15/60 × £12.00 = £3.

(W3) Each unit will absorb the same flat unit rate of £2.50 per unit.

61 HODGSON LTD

Task 1

	Machine hour	Labour hour	Unit
Overheads (£)	250,000	250,000	250,000
Activity	15,000	20,000	100,000
Absorption rate (£)	16.67	12.50	2.50

Task 2

Cost	Machine hour (£)	Labour hour (£)	Unit (£)
Material	24.00	24.00	24.00
Labour	6.00	6.00	6.00
Direct cost	30.00	30.00	30.00
Overheads	5.56	6.25	2.50
Total unit cost	35.56	36.25	32.50

62   BARNES LTD

Task 1

	Machine hour	Labour hour	Unit
Overheads (£)	130,000	130,000	130,000
Activity	17,500	12,000	40,000
Absorption rate (£)	7.43	10.83	3.25

Task 2

Cost	Machine hour (£)	Labour hour (£)	Unit (£)
Material	15.00	15.00	15.00
Labour	5.00	5.00	5.00
Direct cost	20.00	20.00	20.00
Overheads	3.72	3.61	3.25
Total unit cost	23.72	23.61	23.25

63   MAJA LTD

Task 1

	Machine hour	Labour hour	Unit
Overheads (£)	145,000	145,000	145,000
Activity	9,000	11,000	60,000
Absorption rate (£)	16.11	13.18	2.42

Task 2

Cost	Machine hour (£)	Labour hour (£)	Unit (£)
Material	8.00	8.00	8.00
Labour	7.00	7.00	7.00
Direct cost	15.00	15.00	15.00
Overheads	5.37	6.59	2.42
Total unit cost	20.37	21.59	17.42

MANUFACTURING ACCOUNTS

64 JOKER LTD

Manufacturing account – Y/E 31 December

	£
Opening inventory of raw materials	50,000
Purchases of raw materials	120,000
Closing inventory of raw materials	65,000
DIRECT MATERIALS USED	
Direct labour	140,000
DIRECT COST	
Manufacturing overheads	85,000
MANUFACTURING COST	
Opening inventory of work in progress	48,000
Closing inventory of work in progress	52,000
COST OF GOODS MANUFACTURED	
Opening inventory of finished goods	57,000
Closing inventory of finished goods	61,000
COST OF GOODS SOLD	

	£
DIRECT MATERIALS USED	105,000 (W1)
DIRECT COST	245,000 (W2)
MANUFACTURING COST	330,000 (W3)
COST OF GOODS MANUFACTURED	326,000 (W4)
COST OF GOODS SOLD	322,000 (W5)

(W1) Direct materials used = purchases of raw materials + opening raw material inventory – closing raw material inventory = 120,000 + 50,000 – 65,000 = 105,000

(W2) Direct cost = direct materials + direct labour cost = 105,000 (W1) + 140,000 = 245,000

(W3) Manufacturing cost = direct cost + indirect cost of manufacture = 245,000 + 85,000 = 330,000

(W4) Cost of goods manufactured = manufacturing cost + opening inventory of work in progress – closing inventory of work in progress = 330,000 + 48,000 – 52,000 = 326,000

Cost of goods sold = cost of goods manufactured + opening inventory finished goods – closing inventory finished goods = 326,000 + 57,000 – 61,000 = 322,000

65   TUT LTD

Manufacturing account – Y/E 31 July

	£
Opening inventory of raw materials	10,000
Purchases of raw materials	60,000
Closing inventory of raw materials	12,000
DIRECT MATERIALS USED	58,000
Direct labour	88,000
DIRECT COST	146,000
Manufacturing overheads	45,000
MANUFACTURING COST	191,000
Opening inventory of work in progress	12,000
Closing inventory of work in progress	15,000
COST OF GOODS MANUFACTURED	188,000
Opening inventory of finished goods	18,000
Closing inventory of finished goods	20,000
COST OF GOODS SOLD	186,000

	£
DIRECT MATERIALS USED	58,000 (W1)
DIRECT COST	146,000 (W2)
MANUFACTURING COST	191,000 (W3)
COST OF GOODS MANUFACTURED	188,000 (W4)
COST OF GOODS SOLD	186,000 (W5)

(W1) Direct materials used = purchases of raw materials + opening raw material inventory – closing raw material inventory = 60,000 + 10,000 – 12,000 = 58,000

(W2) Direct cost = direct materials + direct labour cost = 58,000 (W1) + 88,000 = 146,000

(W3) Manufacturing cost = direct cost + indirect cost of manufacture = 146,000 + 45,000 = 191,000

(W4) Cost of goods manufactured = manufacturing cost + opening inventory of work in progress – closing inventory of work in progress = 191,000 + 12,000 – 15,000 = 188,000

Cost of goods sold = cost of goods manufactured + opening inventory finished goods – closing inventory finished goods = 188,000 + 18,000 – 20,000 = 186,000

66   RIDDLER LTD

	£
Prime cost	292,000 (W1)
Manufacturing overhead	112,000 (W2)
Total manufacturing cost	404,000 (W3)
Cost of goods manufactured	400,000 (W4)
Cost of goods sold	410,000 (W5)

(W1) Prime cost = direct material cost + direct labour cost = 98,000 (see below) + 194,000

Direct material cost = purchases of raw materials + opening raw material inventory − closing raw material inventory = 100,000 + 20,000 − 22,000 = 98,000

(W2) Manufacturing overhead = indirect materials + indirect labour cost + manufacturing overheads= 25,000 + 12,000 + 75,000 = 112,000

(W3) Manufacturing cost = prime cost + indirect cost of manufacture = 292,000 + 112,000 = 404,000

(W4) Cost of goods manufactured = manufacturing cost + opening inventory of work in progress − closing inventory of work in progress = 404,000 + 31,000 − 35,000 = 400,000

(W5) Cost of goods sold = cost of goods manufactured + opening inventory finished goods − closing inventory finished goods = 400,000 + 60,000 − 50,000 = 410,000

67   CLOCKING LTD

	£
Prime cost	144,000 (W1)
Manufacturing overhead	71,000 (W2)
Total manufacturing cost	215,000 (W3)
Cost of goods manufactured	213,000 (W4)
Cost of goods sold	218,000 (W5)

(W1) Prime cost = direct material cost + direct labour cost = 47,000 (see below) + 97,000

Direct material cost = purchases of raw materials + opening raw material inventory − closing raw material inventory = 50,000 + 7,000 − 10,000 = 47,000

(W2) Manufacturing overhead = indirect materials + indirect labour cost + manufacturing expenses = 8,000 + 10,000 + 53,000 = 71,000

(W3) Manufacturing cost = prime cost + indirect cost of manufacture = 144,000 + 71,000 = 215,000

(W4) Cost of goods manufactured = manufacturing cost + opening inventory of work in progress − closing inventory of work in progress = 215,000 + 8,000 − 10,000 = 213,000

(W5) Cost of goods sold = cost of goods manufactured + opening inventory finished goods − closing inventory finished goods = 213,000 + 30,000 − 25,000 = 218,000

68   BOOKWORM LTD

Manufacturing account – Y/E 31 December

	£
Opening inventory of raw materials	5,000
Purchases of raw materials	15,000
Closing inventory of raw materials	8,000
DIRECT MATERIALS USED	**12,000**
Direct labour	15,000
DIRECT COST	**27,000**
Manufacturing overheads	25,000
MANUFACTURING COST	**52,000**
Opening inventory of work in progress	4,000
Closing inventory of work in progress	(6,000)
COST OF GOODS MANUFACTURED	**50,000**
Opening inventory of finished goods	12,000
Closing inventory of finished goods	(16,000)
COST OF GOODS SOLD	**46,000**

69   MULTI

C – Manufacturing cost + opening WIP – closing WIP + opening FG – closing FG

COSTING FOR INVENTORY AND WORK-IN-PROGRESS

NARRATIVE STYLE QUESTIONS

70   BOBBLE LTD

Characteristic	FIFO	LIFO	AVCO
• Potentially out of date valuation of inventory issues.	✓		
• The valuation of inventory rarely reflects the actual purchase price of the material.			✓
• Potentially out of date closing inventory valuation.		✓	

71   LINT LTD

Statement	True	False
• In periods of rising prices, FIFO gives a higher valuation of closing inventory than LIFO or AVCO.	✓	
• In periods of falling prices, LIFO gives a higher valuation of issues of inventory than FIFO or AVCO.		✓
• AVCO would normally be expected to produce a valuation of closing inventory somewhere between valuations under FIFO and LIFO.	✓	

72   FLUFF LTD

Characteristic	FIFO	LIFO	AVCO
• This inventory valuation method is particularly suited to inventory that consist of liquid materials e.g. oil.			✓
• This inventory valuation method is suited to inventory that has a short shelf life e.g. dairy products.	✓		
• This inventory valuation method is suited to a wheat farmer who has large silos of grain. Grain is added to and taken from the top of these silos.		✓	

73   FIDO LTD

Characteristic	FIFO	LIFO	AVCO
• In times of rising prices this method will give higher profits.	✓		
• In times of rising prices this method will give lower profits.		✓	
• In times of rising prices this method gives a middle level of profits compared to the other two.			✓

74   TRUFFEAUX LTD

Statement	True	False
• FIFO costs issues of inventory at the most recent purchase price.		✓
• AVCO costs issues of inventory at the oldest purchase price.		✓
• LIFO costs issues of inventory at the oldest purchase price.		✓
• FIFO values closing inventory at the most recent purchase price.	✓	
• LIFO values closing inventory at the most recent purchase price.		✓
• AVCO values closing inventory at the latest purchase price.		✓

75   STOCKY LTD

Characteristic	FIFO	LIFO	AVCO
• Issues are valued at the most recent purchase cost.		✓	
• Inventory is valued at the average of the cost of purchases.			✓
• Inventory is valued at the most recent purchase cost.	✓		

IDENTIFICATION OF INVENTORY VALUATION METHOD

76   EPIC LTD

Task 1

Characteristic	FIFO	LIFO	AVCO
• Closing inventory is valued at £28,200.			✓
• The issue of inventory is valued at £67,000.	✓		
• The issue of inventory is valued at £64,000.		✓	

Task 2

	True	False
• AVCO values the issue of inventory at £65,800.	✓	
• LIFO values the closing inventory at £27,000.		✓
• FIFO values the closing inventory at £30,000.		✓

Using FIFO:

Issues will be made from the oldest inventories first. This is the 8,000 units @ £5 per unit (8,000 × £5 = £40,000).

The remaining issue of 6,000 units will be made from the purchase of 12,000 units. This will be 6,000 units @ £4.50 (6,000 × £4.50 = £27,000).

The total issue will be valued at £40,000+£27,000 = £67,000.

The closing inventory will be the remainder of the purchase in the month, which is 6,000 (12,000 – 6,000) units @ £4.50 = £27,000.

Using LIFO:

Issues will be made from the most recent purchase first. This is the 12,000 units @ £4.50 per unit (12,000 × £4.50 = £54,000).

The remaining issue of 2,000 units will be made from the opening inventory valued at £5. This will be 2,000 units @ £5 (2,000 × £5 = £10,000).

The total issue will be valued at £54,000 + £10,000 = £64,000.

The closing inventory will be the remainder of the opening inventory, which is 6,000 units @ £5 = £30,000.

Using AVCO:

The value of the inventory will be averaged. The total number of units is 20,000 units (8,000 + 12,000). The total cost is (8,000 × £5) + (12,000 × £4.50) = £94,000.

The average cost per unit is therefore £94,000/20,000 = £4.70.

The value of the issue will therefore be 14,000 × £4.70 = £65,800.

The closing inventory will also be valued at this average, which will be 6,000 × £4.70 = £28,200.

77 AWESOME LTD

Task 1

Characteristic	FIFO	LIFO	AVCO
• Closing inventory is valued at £48,500.	✓		
• The issue of inventory is valued at £57,200.			✓
• The issue of inventory is valued at £66,900.		✓	

Task 2

	True	False
• FIFO values the issue of inventory at £47,500.	✓	
• AVCO values the closing inventory at £38,400.		✓
• LIFO values the closing inventory at £29,100.	✓	

78   AMAZING LTD

Task 1

Characteristic	FIFO	LIFO	AVCO
• Closing inventory is valued at £1,500.		✓	
• The issue of inventory is valued at £23,000.	✓		
• The issue of inventory is valued at £24,000.			✓

Task 2

	True	False
• LIFO values the issue of inventory at £26,500.	✓	
• AVCO values the closing inventory at £5,000.		✓
• FIFO values the closing inventory at £4,000.		✓

Using FIFO:

Issues will be made from the oldest inventories first. This is the 2,000 units @ £1.50 per unit (2,000 × £1.50 = £3,000).

The remaining issue of 4,000 units will be made from the purchase of 5,000 units. This will be 4,000 units @ £5 (4,000 × £5 = £20,000).

The total issue will be valued at £3,000 + £20,000 = £23,000.

The closing inventory will be the remainder of the purchase in the month, which is 1,000 (5,000-4,000) units @ £5 = £5,000.

Using LIFO:

Issues will be made from the most recent purchase first. This is the 5,000 units @ £5 per unit (5,000 × £5 = £25,000).

The remaining issue of 1,000 units will be made from the opening inventory valued at £1.50. This will be 1,000 units @ £1.50 (1,000 × £1.50 = £1,500).

The total issue will be valued at £25,000 + £1,500 = £26,500.

The closing inventory will be the remainder of the opening inventory, which is 1,000 units @ £1.50 = £1,500.

Using AVCO:

The value of the inventory will be averaged. The total number of units is 7,000 units (2,000 + 5,000). The total cost is (2,000 × £1.50) + (5,000 × £5) = £28,000.

The average cost per unit is therefore £28,000/7,000 = £4.

The value of the issue will therefore be 6,000 × £4 = £24,000.

The closing inventory will also be valued at this average, which will be 1,000 × £4 = £4,000.

INVENTORY CARDS

79   STONE LTD

Method	Cost of issue on 22 June	Closing inventory at 30 June
FIFO	£10,125 **(500 × £15) + (150 × £17.50)**	£17,200 **(£8,750 + £4,950 + £6,125 + £7,500) − £10,125**
LIFO	£11,450 **(275 × £18) + (350 × £17.50) + (25 × £15)**	£15,875 **(£8,750 + £4,950 + £6,125 + £7,500) − £11,450**
AVCO	£10,732 **((£7,500 + £6,125 + £4,950)/ (500 + 350 + 275)) × 650**	£16,593 **(£8,750 + £4,950 + £6,125 + £7,500) − £10,732**

80   NATAL LTD

Task 1

Method	Cost of issue on 2 Dec	Closing inventory at 29 Dec
LIFO	£534,250 **(50,000 × £7) + (14,000 × £8) + (8500 × £8.50)**	£42,750 **(£85,000 + £112,000 + £350,000 + £30,000) − £534,250**
AVCO	£535,912 **((£85,000 + £112,000 + £350,000)/ (10,000 + 14,000 + 50,000)) × 72,500**	£41,088 **(£85,000 + £112,000 + £350,000 + £30,000) − £535,912**

Task 2

	True	False
• FIFO would give a lower closing inventory valuation on the 29th December than LIFO and AVCO.	✓	
• FIFO would give a lower cost of issue on the 25th of December than LIFO and AVCO.		✓

81   GANDALF LTD

	Valuation £
• July 15	£1,030 **(500 × £1.70) + (120 × £1.50)**
• July 31	£660 **(200 × £1.80) + (200 × £1.50)**

82   GRUNDY LTD

Method	Cost of issue on 25 October	Closing inventory at 31 October
FIFO	£20,000 **(6000 × £2.50) + (2500 × £2)**	£5,500
LIFO	£15,250 **(3000 × £1) + (3000 × £2) + (2500 × £2.50)**	£10,250
AVCO	£17,000 **(AVCO = £24,000/12000 units = £2/unit** **Cost of issue = 8500 × £2)**	£8,500

Tutorial note

The quickest way to calculate closing inventory is as total purchases (£25,500) less cost of issues.

83   LOBO LTD

Method	Cost of issue on 29 May	Closing inventory at 30 May
FIFO	£2,500 **(250 × £5.50) + (250 × £4.50)**	£2,250
LIFO	£1,000 **(500 × £2)**	£3,750
AVCO	£1,750 **(AVCO = £4,375/1,250 = £3.50/unit,** **giving cost of issue of 500 × £3.50)**	£3,000

Tutorial note

Quickest to calculate closing inventory as total purchases (£4,750) less cost of issue

84   ZOD LTD

Tutorial note

This question is harder than those seen in the sample assessment but is here to give you more of a challenge!

Method	Cost of issue on 16 Feb	Closing inventory at 26 Feb
FIFO	£290	£905
AVCO (see working below)	£255	£924

AVCO Workings:

DATE	RECEIPTS		ISSUES		BALANCE		
	Units	Cost	Units	Cost	Units	Unit cost	Total cost
February 2	100	£500			100	£5	£500
February 3			50		(50)	(£5)	(£250)
					50	£5	£250
February 12	150	£600			150	£4	£600
					200	£4.25	£850
February 16			60		(60)	(£4.25)	(£255)
					140	(£4.25)	£595
February 20	110	£505			110	£4.59 (to nearest penny)	£505
					250	£4.40	£1,100
February 26			40		(40)	(£4.40)	(£176)
					210	4.40	£924

COSTING FOR LABOUR

NARRATIVE STYLE QUESTIONS

85   NULAB LTD

Payment method	Time-rate	Piecework	Piece-rate plus bonus
• Labour is paid based on the production achieved.		✓	
• Labour is paid extra if an agreed level of output is exceeded.			✓
• Labour is paid according to hours worked.	✓		

86 LU LTD

Payment method	Time-rate	Piecework	Time-rate plus bonus
• Assured level of remuneration for employee.	✓		
• Employee earns more if they work more efficiently than expected.		✓	
• Assured level of remuneration and reward for working efficiently.			✓

87 MANDELA LTD

Statement	True	False
• Time rate is paid based on the production achieved.		✓
• Overtime is paid for hours worked over the standard hours agreed.	✓	
• Piece rate is paid according to hours worked.		✓

88 PERRES LTD

Payment method	Basic rate	Overtime premium	Overtime rate
• This is the amount paid above the basic rate for hours worked in excess of the normal hours.		✓	
• This is the total amount paid per hour for hours worked in excess of the normal hours.			✓
• This is the amount paid per hour for normal hours worked.	✓		

89 TEVEZ LTD

Statement	True	False
• Direct labour costs can be identified with the goods being made or the service being provided.	✓	
• Indirect labour costs vary directly with the level of activity.		✓

90   BERDYCH LTD

Payment method	Variable	Fixed
• Labour that is paid based on a time rate basis per hour worked.	✓	
• Labour is paid on a monthly salary basis.		✓
• Labour that is based on number of units produced.	✓	

91   SODERLING LTD

Payment method	Time-rate	Piecework	Salary
• Assured level of remuneration for employee usually agreed for the year.			✓
• Employee earnings are directly linked with units they produce.		✓	
• Employee earnings are directly linked with hours they work.	✓		

92   MURRAY LTD

	True	False
• Indirect labour costs includes production supervisors' salaries.	✓	
• Direct labour costs usually vary directly with the level of activity.	✓	

93   OWEN LTD

Payment method	Time-rate	Piecework	Salary
• Employee is paid the same amount every month.			✓
• Employee wage increases in direct correlation with the number of hours worked.	✓		
• Employee wage increases in direct correlation with the number of units produced.		✓	

94   PIECEWORK STATEMENTS

Statement	True	False
• Piecework encourages employees to work harder.	✓	
• Piecework requires accurate recording of the number of hours staff have worked.		✓
• Piecework encourages workers to improve the quality of the units they produce.		✓

CALCULATING LABOUR COSTS

95   MUTANT LTD

Worker	Hours worked	Basic wage	Overtime	Gross wage
S. Torm (W1)	34 hours	£240	£23	£263
J. Grey (W2)	38 hours	£240	£68	£308

(W1) Basic wage is based on 32 hour week = 32 × £7.50 = £240

Overtime is paid at time and a half (£7.50 × 1.5 = £11.25) = (34-32) hours × £11.25 = £23

(W1) Basic wage is based on 32 hour week = 32 × £7.50 = £240

Overtime is paid at time and a half (£7.50 × 1.5 = £11.25) = (38-32) hours × £11.25 = £68

96   PHOENIX LTD

Statement	True	False
An employee who works 38 hours and makes 775 units will not receive a bonus. (W1)		✓
An employee who works 40 hours and makes 815 units will receive total pay of £342.50. (W2)	✓	
An employee who works 37 hours and makes 744 units will earn a bonus of £6. (W3)	✓	

(W1) In 38 hours a worker should make 38 × 20 = 760 units. If a worker made 775 units, this is 15 units above the expectation, and so a bonus would be paid.

(W2) In 40 hours a worker should make 40 × 20 = 800 units. If a worker made 815 units, this is 15 units above the expectation. The bonus will therefore be 15 × £1.50 = £22.50. The basic wage will be 40 hours @ £8 = £320. The total pay will therefore be £320 + £22.50 = £342.50.

(W3) In 37 hours a worker should make 37 × 20 = 740 units. If a worker made 744 units, this is 4 units above the expectation. The bonus will therefore be 4 × £1.50 = £6.

97   KAHN LTD

Worker	Hours worked	Units produced	Basic wage	Bonus	Gross wage
A. Smith (W1)	35	175	£420	£0	£420
J. O'Hara (W2)	35	180	£420	£6	£426
M.Stizgt (W3)	35	185	£420	£12	£432

(W1) In 35 hours a worker should make 35 × 5 = 175 units. No bonus will be paid.

(W2) In 35 hours a worker should make 35 × 5 = 175 units. If 180 units are made, this is 5 units above expectation. If 5 units can be made in 1 hour this is equivalent to 1 hour's work. The bonus will therefore be 1 × £6 = £6.

(W3) If a worker made 185 units, this is 10 units above the expectation. If 5 units can be made in 1 hour this is equivalent to 2 hour's work. The bonus will therefore be 2 × £6 = £12.

98   ENTERPRISE LTD

Bonus calculation	Correct	Incorrect
Javier produced 400 units and earned a bonus of £6. (W1)		✓
Esha produced 465 units and earned a bonus of £390. (W2)		✓
Mika produced 480 units and earned a bonus of £300. (W3)	✓	

(W1) The bonus is paid for every unit in excess of 400 units, therefore beginning at unit 401. No bonus will be paid for the 400th unit.

(W2) If 465 units are produced, this is 65 more than the target. However, the bonus is capped at 450 units. Therefore the bonus will only be received for units 401–450 (i.e. 50 units). The maximum bonus achievable is therefore 50 × £6 = £300.

(W3) If 480 units are produced, this is 80 more than the target. However, the bonus is capped at 450 units. Therefore the bonus will only be received for units 401–450 (i.e. 50 units). The maximum bonus achievable is therefore 50 × £6 = £300.

99   SGC LTD

Worker	Units produced in week	Gross wage
J. O'Neill	500 units	£660.00 (W1)
S. Carter	650 units	£772.50 (W2)

(W1) Basic salary = £285. If 500 units are produced this will be paid at £0.75 × 500 = £375. Gross wage = £285 + £375 = £660.

(W2) Basic salary = £285. If 650 units are produced this will be paid at £0.75 × 650 = £487.50 Gross wage = £285 + £487.50 = £772.50.

100   GOTHIC LTD

Pay calculation	Correct	Incorrect
M. Shelley worked for 35 hours and earned total income of £595. (W1)		✓
G. Leroux worked for 37 hours and earned total income of £929.	✓	
A.E. Poe worked for 32 hours and earned total income of £874.		✓
The total bonus paid by Gothic Ltd was £1,500.	✓	

Production target = 20,000 units. Actual output = 22,100 units. This is an increase of 2,100 units, with a percentage increase of 2,100/20,000 × 100 = 10.5% (therefore 10 complete percent). The bonus will therefore be 10 × £30 = £300 for each employee.

(W1) Basic wage = 35 × £17 = £595. Plus bonus of £300 = £895.

(W2) Basic wage = 37 × £17 = £629. Plus bonus of £300 = 929.

(W3) Basic wage = 32 × £17 = £544. Plus bonus of £300 = 844.

(W4) Total bonus = £300 × 5 employees = £1,500.

101   AVENGERS LTD

Worker	Hours worked	Basic wage	Overtime	Gross wage
T. Stark	138	£1,380	£0	£1,380
B. Banner	142	£1,400	£25	£1,425
S. Rogers	145	£1,400	£63	£1,463

102   DRACO LTD

Worker	Units produced in week	Gross wage
P. Jones	240 units	£192 (W1)
D. Bannatyne	350 units	£250 (W2)
L. Redford	250 units	£200 (W3)

(W1) No units produced above standard, therefore all are paid at £0.80 (240 × £0.80 = £192).

(W2) 100 units above standard are made (350-250). These are paid a bonus of £10 per 20 units. This is therefore a bonus of 100/20 × £10 = £50. Standard production is all paid at £0.80 which is therefore £0.80 × 250 = £200. Gross wage = £200 + £50 = £250.

(W3) No units above the standard are made. The bonus does not start until unit 251. Standard production is all paid at £0.80 which is therefore £0.80 × 250 = £200.

103 QUAGGA PLC

Statement	True	False
During a 29 hour week, an employee producing 1,475 units would not receive a bonus.		✓
During a 32 hour week, an employee producing 1,665 units would receive a bonus of £29.25.	✓	
During a 37 hour week, an employee producing 1,925 units would receive total pay of £300.25.		✓

104 JLA PLC

Statement	True	False
During a 30 hour week, an employee producing 192 units would receive a bonus of £16.	✓	
During a 35 hour week, an employee producing 240 units would receive total pay of £215.	✓	
During a 30 hour week, an employee producing 180 units would not receive a bonus.	✓	

105 INJUSTICE LTD

Worker	Units produced	Basic wage	Piece work	Gross wage
N. Wing	295	£175	£354	£529
W. Woman	355	£175	£426	£601
T. Flash	385	£175	£462	£637

106 GREENWOOD LTD

Worker	Hours worked	Units produced	Basic wage	Bonus	Gross wage
B. Ryan	35	175	£350	£0	£350
S. Chang	35	190	£350	£21	£371
E. Schneider	35	210	£350	£49	£399

VARIANCES

NARRATIVE QUESTIONS

107 VARIOUS LTD

Statement	True	False
• A variance is the difference between budgeted and actual cost.	✓	
• A favourable variance means actual costs are less than budgeted.	✓	
• An adverse variance means that actual income is less than budgeted.	✓	
• A favourable variance occurs when actual income is the same as budgeted income.		✓

108 JONES LTD

Statement	True	False
If budgeted sales are 6,000 units at £7.50 per unit and actual sales are £47,600, the sales variance is favourable (W1)	✓	
A favourable cost variance occurs when an actual cost of £9,800 is compared to a budgeted cost of £24 per unit for a budgeted output of 400 units (W2)		✓
A variance arises from a comparison of budgeted costs for last year with actual costs for this year		✓
If actual material costs are the same as budgeted costs for materials then no variance arises	✓	

(W1) Sales variance = actual sales – budgeted sales = £47,600 – (6,000 × £7.50) = £2,600.

As actual sales are greater than budgeted, the income will be greater, and the variance is favourable.

(W2) If budgeted costs for 400 units are £24 each, this is a total budget of £9,600. If actual costs are £9,800 then this means we have incurred more costs than planned. This is therefore an adverse variance as profits will be reduced.

109 GATLAND LTD

Statement	True	False
If budgeted sales are 4,000 units at £9.50 per unit and actual sales are £35,200, the sales variance is favourable		✓
A favourable cost variance occurs when an actual cost of £6,400 is compared to a budgeted cost of £14 per unit for a budgeted output of 500 units	✓	
A variance arises from a comparison of budgeted costs for last year with budgeted costs for this year		✓
If actual material costs are the same as budgeted costs for materials then the materials variance is adverse		✓

(W1) Sales variance = actual sales – budgeted sales = £35,200 – (4,000 × £9.50) = (£2,800).

As actual sales are less than budgeted, the income will be lower, and the variance is adverse.

(W2) If budgeted costs for 500 units are £14 each, this is a total budget of £7,000. If actual costs are £6,400 then this means we have incurred less costs than planned. This is therefore a favourable variance as profits will be increased.

110 LANCASTER LTD

Statement	True	False
If budgeted sales are 14,000 units at £3.50 per unit and actual sales are £45,200, the sales variance is favourable		✓
An adverse cost variance occurs when an actual cost of £68,400 is compared to a budgeted cost of £14 per unit for a budgeted output of 5,000 units		✓
A variance arises from a comparison of budgeted costs for this year with actual costs for this year	✓	
If actual material costs are the same as budgeted costs for materials then the materials variance is favourable		✓

111 GOODE LTD

Statement	True	False
The variance for the Direct Material cost of Department B should be reported to the purchasing manager	✓	
The variance for the Direct Labour cost for Department A should be reported to the sales manager		✓
The variance for the Direct Labour cost for Department B should be reported to the production manager of Department A		✓
A Direct Material cost variance that has been deemed Not Significant should not be reported	✓	

112 BROWN LTD

Statement	True	False
The variance for the Direct Material cost of Department A should be reported to the purchasing manager	✓	
The variance for the Direct Labour cost for Department A should be reported to the production manager of Department B		✓
The variance for sales should be reported to the sales manager	✓	
A Direct Material cost variance that has been deemed Significant should not be reported		✓

VARIANCE CALCULATION QUESTIONS

113 EREBOR LTD

Cost type	Budget £	Actual £	Variance £	Adverse or favourable (A or F)
Sales	600,500	597,800	2,700	A
Direct materials	205,800	208,500	2,700	A
Direct labour	155,000	154,800	200	F
Production overheads	65,000	72,100	7,100	A
Administration overheads	58,400	55,200	3,200	F

114 MORIA LTD

Cost type	Budget	Variance	Variance as % of budget	Significant or Not significant
Sales	45,100	4,214	9 (W1)	S
Material	15,750	1,260	8 (W2)	S
Labour	12,915	805	6	NS
Variable overheads	5,750	315	5	NS
Fixed overheads	8,155	1,011	12	S

(W1) Variance as % = variance / budget × 100 = 4,214/45,100 × 100 = 9 %

(W2) Variance as % = variance / budget × 100 = 1,260/15,750 × 100 = 8 %

115 WYEDALE LTD

Cost type	Budget £	Actual £	Variance £	Variance %	Adverse/ Favourable
Sales	27,000	29,775	2,775	10	F
Direct materials	7,400	8,510	1,110	15	A
Direct labour	7,200	7,920	720	10	A
Production overheads	5,500	5,390	110	2	F
Administration overheads	4,500	4,365	135	3	F

Variance as % = variance / budget × 100

116   BELEGOST LTD

	Budget £	Actual £	Adverse or Favourable (A or F)	Significant or Not significant (S or NS)
Sales	205,000	207,100	F	NS
Direct materials	75,150	78,750	A	NS
Direct labour	110,556	107,950	F	NS
Production overheads	14,190	12,500	F	S
Non-production overheads	16,190	17,880	A	S

Variance as % = variance / budget × 100

117   IVAN LTD

Cost type	Budget £	Actual £	Variance £	Adverse or favourable (A or F)
Sales	544,750	547,450	2,700	F
Direct materials	76,800	80,200	3,400	A
Direct labour	148,400	146,000	2,400	F
Production overheads	136,000	144,200	8,200	A
Administration overheads	105,000	109,800	4,800	A

118   BLUEBELL LTD

Cost type	Budget £	Actual £	Variance £	Adverse/ Favourable	%
Sales	£204,555	£197,455	7,100	A	3
Direct materials	£39,000	£42,300	3,300	A	8
Direct labour	£75,000	£83,000	8,000	A	11
Production overheads	£69,000	£64,800	4,200	F	6
Administration overheads	£53,000	£58,900	5,900	A	11

119 TELMAH LTD

Cost type	Budget £	Actual £	Variance £	Variance %	Significant/ not significant	Report to
Sales (W1)	310,000	353,400	43,400	14.00	S	DM
Fuel costs (W2)	25,000	31,250	6,250	25.00	S	DD
Entertaining (W3)	16,000	15,500	500	3.13	NS	-

(W1) Sales variance = 353,400 – 310,000 = 43,400.

Percentage variance = 43,400/310,000 × 100 = 14%. This is a favourable variance and so bullet point 2 does not apply. It is less than 20% and so bullet point 3 does not apply. It is greater than 5% and greater than £500 and so is significant and should be reported to the department manager.

(W2) Fuel costs variance = 31,250 – 25,000 = 6,250.

Percentage variance = 6,250/31,250 × 100 = 25%. This is an adverse variance and bullet points 2 and 3 apply and so is significant. It should therefore be reported to the department director.

(W3) Entertaining variance = 15,500 – 16,000 = 500.

Percentage variance = 500/16,000 × 100 = 3.13%. This is a favourable variance and so bullet point 2 does not apply. It is less than 20% and so bullet point 3 does not apply. It is greater than 5%, but less than £500 and so is not significant and does not need to be reported to anyone.

Section 3

MOCK – QUESTIONS

TASK 1.1

(a) **(i)** **Select TWO of the descriptions used when classifying costs by element from the list below by dragging them into the answer box.** **(2 marks)**

Answer	Variable	Fixed
	Direct	Indirect
	Labour	Materials

(ii) **Complete the following sentences using the drop-down lists.** **(2 marks)**

Costs where the average cost per unit is constant at any activity level, are known as

[▽]

Drop-downs:

variable costs.
stepped costs.
fixed costs.
semi-variable.

When a manufacturing business classifies costs by element for production, planned overtime would be recorded as

[▽]

Drop-downs:

labour.
materials.
overheads.

(b) **Identify whether the following statements are true or false.** **(2 marks)**

Statement	True	False
Management accounts may be presented in any format required by managers.		
Financial accounts are prepared on historical information.		

Wellgone Ltd, a firm of consultants, uses an alphanumeric coding system to allocate costs.

(c) **(i)** **Code the following transactions for the project, using the table below. Each transaction should have a six character code.** **(2 marks)**

Activity	Code	Sub-class	Sub code		Transaction	Code
Revenue	REV	IT consultancy	100		Marketing telephone costs	
		HR consultancy	200		HR consultancy sales	
Consultancy costs	CON	Wages	100			
		Admin support	200			
Marketing	MAR	Telephone	324			
		Wages	345			

(ii) **Identify whether the following statements are true or false using the drop-down list below.** **(2 marks)**

A manufacturing account shows the total manufacturing cost during an accounting period.

∇

Drop-downs

True
False

In a manufacturing account the closing inventory of finished goods needs to be added to determine the cost of goods sold.

∇

Drop-downs

True
False

TASK 1.2

(a) **Identify whether the following statements are true or false.** **(2 marks)**

Statement	True	False
FIFO uses the oldest values of purchases to value closing inventories.		
LIFO uses the oldest values of purchases to value inventory issues.		

(b) **(i)** **Identify the labour costing methods described below using the drop down list.**

(1 mark)

Labour costs are calculated by multiplying a basic rate by the number of items produced, subject to a minimum wage earned each week.

Drop-downs

Piece rate
Time rate
Time rate with bonus
Piece rate with guarantee
Time rate with overtime

(ii) **Identify whether the following statement is true or false using the drop-down list.**

(1 mark)

Businesses paying using the time-rate method must offer overtime.

Drop-downs

True
False

(c) **Identify TWO ways in which information on forecast costs is used by clicking on the left-hand box and matching it to the appropriate right-hand boxes. You can remove a line by clicking on it.** **(2 marks)**

	To prepare annual accounts
	To value inventory
Uses for forecast costs	To classify cost elements
	To help set unit sales prices
	To enable management to monitor performance

(d) Identify TWO examples of cost centres and ONE example of a profit centre for a manufacturing business from the items below by dragging them into the appropriate answer box. **(3 marks)**

Cost centre	Profit centre

Research department	Sales division
Administration costs	Maintenance department
Sales director wages	Raw materials

(e) In a manufacturing business that only makes one product the most appropriate overhead absorption method would be: **(1 mark)**

∇

Drop-down

Per unit
Per labour hour
Per machine hour

TASK 1.3

Fandom Ltd uses the last in first out (LIFO) method of inventory control.

One receipt and one issue of raw material SL4 were made during the first half of April. These are shown in the inventory record below:

(a) **Complete the inventory record below for the receipt and issue of SL4 during April, and calculate closing balance at 25 April.**

The cost per kg entries should be completed in pounds (£) to THREE decimal places.

(6 marks)

Date	Receipt			Issue			Balance	
	Quantity (kg)	Cost per kg (£)	Total cost (£)	Quantity (kg)	Cost per kg (£)	Total cost (£)	Quantity (kg)	Total cost (£)
Balance at 1 April							3,000	4,500
10 April	12,000		21,600					
25 April				10,800			4,200	

(b) **Identify the cost of the issue on 25 April and closing inventory balance if Fandom Ltd had used the weighted average cost (AVCO) or first in first out (FIFO) methods instead.**

(4 marks)

Using AVCO the cost of the issue would be £ ▽ and the closing inventory balance: £ ▽

16,200
18,540
18,792

7,308
7,560
9,900

Using FIFO the cost of the issue would be £ ▽ and the closing inventory balance: £ ▽

16,200
18,540
18,792

7,308
7,560
9,900

TASK 1.4

A company pays its employees a basic rate of £8 per hour for a 32.5 hour working week (Monday to Friday).

Any overtime during the week is paid at time and a half (basic pay + 50%).

Any weekend working is paid at double time (2 × basic pay).

(a) Calculate the basic pay, overtime and gross pay for the week for an employee working the hours shown below.

All hours worked are paid at basic rate with the overtime premiums being the increased pay only. **(4 marks)**

Hours worked Monday to Friday	Hours worked at the weekend	Basic pay £	Overtime premium earned during week £	Overtime premium earning at weekends £	Gross pay £
34	9				

The company has a production target of 400 units for each production employee. Any excess production is rewarded by a bonus of £6 per unit, capped at a maximum production of 450 units.

(b) Identify whether the bonus calculations for the following employees are correct or incorrect. **(4 marks)**

Bonus calculation	Correct	Incorrect
Employee 1 produces 360 units and earns a bonus of £0.		
Employee 2 produces 400 units and earns a bonus of £6.		
Employee 3 produces 420 units and earns a bonus of £120.		
Employee 4 produces 460 units and earns a bonus of £360.		

TASK 1.5

Frodo Ltd is considering how to cost the various products it makes. It needs to decide on the overhead absorption basis it will use. The methods it is considering are:

- a machine hour basis

- a labour hour basis

- a per unit basis

(a) **Complete the table below to show the three overhead absorption rates that Frodo Ltd could use. Show your calculations to two decimal places.** (3 marks)

	Machine hour	Labour hour	Unit
Overheads (£)	180,000	180,000	180,000
Activity	26,866	45,000	60,000
Absorption rate (£)			

(b) **Complete the table below to calculate the total unit cost of product GT7. Use each of the three overhead absorption rates you calculated in (a). Show your calculations to two decimal places.** (6 marks)

Each unit of GT7 takes 30 minutes of machine time and 10 minutes of labour time to produce.

	Machine hour (£)	Labour hour (£)	Unit (£)
Direct cost	32.65	32.65	32.65
Overheads			
Total unit cost			

(c) **Which of the three overhead recovery methods would best be suited to an automated production line?** (1 mark)

∇

Drop down

Machine hours
Labour hours
Per unit

TASK 1.6

A manager needs to understand how the costs of the company's single product change at different output levels.

(a) **Complete the table below to separate out the variable and fixed costs of the product.**

(6 marks)

Note: You should use the high-low method to divide the total costs into their variable and fixed elements.

Units	Total costs £	Variable costs £	Fixed costs £
6,000	12,000		
7,500	12,600		
12,000	14,400		

(b) **Identify the correct cost behaviour for the four costs shown below.** **(4 marks)**

Cost behaviour	Fixed	Variable	Semi-variable	Step-fixed
The cost is fixed for a limited output range and then increases.				
The unit cost is the same whatever the output level.				
The cost consists of a part that stays the same and a part that changes with the output level.				
The total cost is the same whatever the output level				

TASK 1.7

Barbara Ltd has the following information for its last quarter:

	£
Materials costs:	
Materials forming part of product	36,000
Materials not forming part of product	4,000
Labour costs:	
Labour working on production	10,000
Labour supporting work on production	34,000
Factory indirect expenses	26,000

Relevant inventory changes were as below:

	£
Work in progress:	
Opening	3,000
Closing	12,000
Finished goods:	
Opening	14,000
Closing	12,000

Complete the table below to show Barbara Ltd's cost structure for the last quarter. **(8 marks)**

Cost structure for the last quarter	£
Direct materials cost	
Direct labour costs	
Manufacturing overhead	
Total manufacturing cost	
Cost of goods manufactured	
Cost of goods sold	

TASK 1.8

All eight production employees in a company are paid a basic £16 per hour for a 35 hour working week (Monday to Friday).

Any overtime during the week is paid at time and a half (basic pay + 50%).

Any weekend working is paid at double time (2 × basic pay).

(a)   Calculate the basic pay, overtime and gross pay for the week for each employee working the hours shown below. (Note: All hours worked are paid at basic rate with the overtime premiums being the increased pay only). **(4 marks)**

Hours worked Monday to Friday	Hours worked at the weekend	Basic pay £	Overtime premium earned during week £	Overtime premium earned at weekends £	Gross pay £
36	8				

Each employee has a production target of 2,000 units per month. All production in excess of this is rewarded by a bonus of £0.30 per additional unit. Last month 3,000 units were produced per employee

(b)   Complete the following sentence. **(1 mark)**

Last month each employee was paid a bonus of: £ [   ]

The gross pay for each employee was the same as you calculated in (a) in each of the four weeks last month.

(c)   Complete the following sentence. **(1 mark)**

Last month the total pay including bonuses for ALL eight production employees was: £ [   ]

(d)   (i)   Calculate the total cost and cost per unit of last month's production.

(ii)   Calculate what these figures would have been if production had increased to 25,440 units. **(8 marks)**

Notes:

1   The direct labour cost for the production of 24,000 units is your figure calculated in part (b) above.

2   Calculate the costs per unit to three decimal places.

Units produced and sold	24,000	25,440
	£	£
Variable costs:		
Direct Materials	22,800	
Direct labour		
Fixed costs:		
Manufacturing overheads	45,000	
Total cost		
Cost per unit		

TASK 1.9

The production cost centre of a factory spent £1,600 more on raw materials than was budgeted and £800 less than was budgeted on wages.

(a) **(i)** **Complete the table below to show the actual expense and identify whether the variance was adverse or favourable.** **(4 marks)**

	Budgeted expense	Actual expense incurred	Adverse/ Favourable
	£	£	
Raw materials	16,350		▽
Wages	12,725		▽

Drop down

Adverse
Favourable

(ii) **Identify whether the following statement is true or false by using the tick boxes below.** **(1 mark)**

Statement	True	False
A company that has a favourable variance on sales has received less income than budgeted.		

You are reviewing the performance of the IT department. The variance on operating costs was 5% below the budgeted figure.

(b) **Complete the table below to show the variance and actual expense, and identify whether the variance was adverse or favourable.** **(3 marks)**

	Budgeted expense	Variance	Adverse/ Favourable	Actual expense
	£	£		£
IT operational costs	13,600		▽	

Drop down

Adverse
Favourable

TASK 1.10

You have been asked to provide information on the company performance report for the month. The budgeted and actual figures have already been summarised in the information below.

	Budgeted £	Actual £
Quality control costs	147,000	135,700

(a) **(i)** **Calculate the variance on quality control costs.** **(1 mark)**

£ _____

(ii) **Calculate the percentage quality control costs variance to TWO decimal places.** **(1 mark)**

_____ %

(iii) **Identify whether the variance is favourable or adverse using the drop-down list.** **(1 mark)**

_____ ▽

Drop down

Adverse
Favourable

You have been provided with variance information by your assistant.

Reporting policies state that

- Variances in excess of 5% of budget, and that are greater than £500, are significant. They should be reported to the department manager.

- Adverse variances in excess of 10% of budget, and that are greater than £1,000, are significant. They should be reported to the department director.

- Any variances in excess of 20% of budget, and that are greater than £2,000, are significant. They should be reported to the department director.

(b) Complete the table below to show each variance percentage. Identify whether the variance is significant or not, and who (if anyone) the information should be reported to.

Percentages should be to TWO decimal places. **(9 marks)**

	Budgeted income/expense £	Actual income/ expense incurred £	Variance £	Variance as percentage of budget %	Significant/ not significant	Report to
Sales	150,000	166,000	16,000		▽	▽
Telephone	4,600	5,025	425		▽	▽
Production wages	125,200	148,800	23,600		▽	▽

LH Drop downs

Significant
Not significant

RH drop downs

Departmental manager
Not required
Department director

Section 4

MOCK – ANSWERS

TASK 1.1

(a) **(i)** Select TWO of the descriptions used when classifying costs by element from the list below by dragging them into the answer box. **(2 marks)**

Labour
Materials

(ii) Complete the following sentences using the drop-down lists. **(2 marks)**

Costs where the average cost per unit is constant at any activity level, are known as | variable costs.

When a manufacturing business classifies costs by element for production, planned overtime would be recorded as | labour.

(b) Identify whether the following statements are true or false. **(2 marks)**

Statement	True	False
Management accounts may be presented in any format required.	X	
Financial accounts are prepared on historical information.	X	

(c) **(i)** Code the following transactions for the project. **(2 marks)**

Transaction	Code
Marketing telephone costs	MAR324
HR consultancy sales	REV200

(ii) Identify whether the following statements are true or false. **(2 marks)**

A manufacturing account shows the total manufacturing cost during an accounting period.

True

In a manufacturing account the closing inventory of finished goods needs to be added to determine the cost of goods sold.

False

TASK 1.2

(a) Identify whether the following statements are true or false. **(2 marks)**

Statement	True	False
FIFO uses the oldest values of purchases to value closing inventories.		X
LIFO uses the oldest values of purchases to value inventory issues.		X

(b) **(ii)** Identify the labour costing methods described below using the drop down list. **(1 mark)**

Labour costs are calculated by multiplying a basic rate by the number of items produced, subject to a minimum wage earned each week. | Piece rate with guarantee

(ii) Identify whether the following statement is true or false using the drop-down list. **(1 mark)**

Businesses paying using the time-rate method must offer overtime. | False ▽

(c) Identify TWO ways in which information on forecast costs is used by clicking on the left-hand box and matching it to the appropriate right-hand boxes. You can remove a line by clicking on it. **(2 marks)**

To help set unit sales prices

To enable management to monitor performance

(d) Identify TWO examples of cost centres and ONE example of a profit centre for a manufacturing business from the items below by dragging them into the appropriate answer box. **(3 marks)**

Cost centre	Profit centre
Research department	Sales division
Maintenance department	

(e) In a manufacturing business that only makes one product the most appropriate overhead absorption method would be: **(1 mark)**

Per unit ▽

TASK 1.3

(a) Complete the inventory record below for the receipt and issue of SL4 during April, and calculate closing balance at 25 April. (6 marks)

Date	Receipt			Issue			Balance	
	Quantity (kg)	Cost per kg (£)	Total cost (£)	Quantity (kg)	Cost per kg (£)	Total cost (£)	Quantity (kg)	Total cost (£)
Balance at 1 April							3,000	4,500
10 April	12,000	1.800	21,600				15,000	26,100
25 April				10,800	1.800	19,440	4,200	6,660

(b) Identify the cost of the issue on 25 April and closing inventory balance if Fandom Ltd had used the weighted average cost (AVCO) or first in first out (FIFO) methods instead.

(4 marks)

Using AVCO the cost of the issue would be £ [∇]

16,200
18,540
18,792

and the closing inventory balance: £ [∇]

7,308
7,560
9,900

Using FIFO the cost of the issue would be £ [∇]

16,200
18,540
18,792

and the closing inventory balance: £ [∇]

7,308
7,560
9,900

AVCO

- Before April 25 we had a total of 15,000 kgs (3,000 b/f + 12,000 receipt) at a total cost of £4,500 + £21,600 = £26,100
- On average this works out at £26,100/15,000 = £1.74 per kg
- Thus the cost of the issue will be 10,800 × £1.74 = £18,792
- Closing inventory = £26,100 - £18,792 = £7,308

FIFO

- The issue will be made up of all 3,000 kgs b/f and 7,800 kg from the receipt on 10 April
- Thus the cost of issue = £4,500 + £14,040 + (7,800 × £1.80) = £18,540
- Closing inventory = £26,100 – £18,540 = £7,560

TASK 1.4

(a)   Calculate the basic pay, overtime and gross pay for the week for an employee working the hours shown below.

All hours worked are paid at basic rate with the overtime premiums being the increased pay only.   (4 marks)

Hours worked Monday to Friday	Hours worked at the weekend	Basic pay £	Overtime premium earned during week £	Overtime premium earning at weekends £	Gross pay £
34	9	344	6	72	422

(b)   Identify whether the bonus calculations for the following employees are correct or incorrect.   (4 marks)

Bonus calculation	Correct	Incorrect
Employee 1 produces 360 units and earns a bonus of £0.	X	
Employee 2 produces 400 units and earns a bonus of £6.		X
Employee 3 produces 420 units and earns a bonus of £120.	X	
Employee 4 produces 460 units and earns a bonus of £360.		X

TASK 1.5

(a)   Complete the table below to show the three overhead absorption rates that Frodo Ltd could use. Show your calculations to two decimal places.   (3 marks)

	Machine hour	Labour hour	Unit
Overheads (£)	180,000	180,000	180,000
Activity	26,866	45,000	60,000
Absorption rate (£)	6.70	4.00	3.00

OAR = budgeted overheads / budgeted activity level

(b)   Complete the table below to calculate the total unit cost of product GT7. Use each of the three overhead absorption rates you calculated in (a).   (6 marks)

	Machine hour (£)	Labour hour (£)	Unit (£)
Direct cost	32.65	32.65	32.65
Overheads	3.35 (W1)	0.67	3.00
Total unit cost	36.00	33.32	35.65

(W1) Overhead per unit = 30 minutes (30/60 hours) × £6.70 = £3.35

(W2) Overhead per unit = 10 minutes (10/60 hours) × £4.00 = £0.67

(c)   Which of the three overhead recovery methods would best be suited to an automated production line?   **(1 mark)**

Machine hours ∇

TASK 1.6

(a)   Complete the table below to separate out the variable and fixed costs of the product.
(6 marks)

Units	Total costs £	Variable costs £	Fixed costs £
6,000	12,000	2,400 (W1)	9,600
7,500	12,600	3,000	9,600
12,000	14,400	4,800	9,600

Using high-low method:

Variable cost per unit   = cost at highest activity level – cost at lowest activity level

highest activity level – lowest activity level

= £14,400 - £12,000

12,000 – 6,000

= £0.40 per unit

Substitute variable cost per unit back into total cost for 6,000 units to find fixed cost:

Fixed cost   = total cost – variable cost

= £12,000 – (£0.40 x 6,000)

= £9,600

(W1) Variable cost = activity level x variable cost per unit = 6,000 x £0.40 = £2,400.

(b)   Identify the correct cost behaviour for the four costs shown below.   **(4 marks)**

Cost behaviour	Fixed	Variable	Semi-variable	Step fixed
The cost is fixed for a limited output range and then increases.				X
The unit cost is the same whatever the output level.		X		
The cost consists of a part that stays the same and a part that changes with the output level.			X	
The total cost is the same whatever the output level	X			

TASK 1.7

Complete the table below to show Barbara Ltd's cost structure for the last quarter. **(8 marks)**

Cost structure for the last quarter	£
Direct materials cost	36,000
Direct labour costs	10,000
Manufacturing overhead	64,000 (W1)
Total manufacturing cost	110,000 (W2)
Cost of goods manufactured	101,000 (W3)
Cost of goods sold	103,000 (W4)

(W1) Manufacturing overhead = indirect materials + indirect labour + indirect factory expenses
= £4,000 + £34,000 + £26,000 = £64,000
(W2) Total manufacturing cost = £36,000 + £10,000 + £64,000 = £110,000
(W3) Cost of goods manufactured = total manufacturing cost + opening WIP − closing WIP
= £110,000 + £3,000 - £12,000 = £101,000
(W4) Cost of goods sold = cost of goods manufactured + opening finished − closing finished
= £101,000 + £14,000 - £12,000 = £103,000

TASK 1.8

(a) **Calculate the basic pay, overtime and gross pay for the week for each employee working the hours shown below. (Note: All hours worked are paid at basic rate with the overtime premiums being the increased pay only).** **(4 marks)**

Hours worked Monday to Friday	Hours worked at the weekend	Basic pay £	Overtime premium earned during week £	Overtime premium earned at weekends £	Gross pay £
36	8	704	8	128	840

(b) **Complete the following sentence.** **(1 mark)**

Last month each employee was paid a bonus of: £ 300

(c) **Complete the following sentence.** **(1 mark)**

Last month the total pay including bonuses for ALL eight production employees was: £ 29,280

(d) **(i)** Calculate the total cost and cost per unit of last month's production.

(ii) Calculate what these figures would have been if production had increased to 25,440 units. **(8 marks)**

Units produced and sold	24,000	25,440
	£	£
Variable costs:		
Direct Materials	22,800	24,168 (W1)
Direct labour	29,280	31,037 (W2)
Fixed costs:		
Manufacturing overheads	45,000	45,000
Total cost	97,080	100,205
Cost per unit	4.045	3.939

(W1) Direct materials cost per unit = £22,800/24,000 units = £0.95 per unit
For 25,440 units = £0.95 × 25,440 = £24,168

(W2) Direct labour cost per unit = £29,280/24,000 units = £1.22 per unit
For 25,440 units = £1.22 × 25,440 = £31,036.80 (round up to £31,037)

TASK 1.9

(a) **(i)** Complete the table below to show the actual expense and identify whether the variance was adverse or favourable. **(4 marks)**

	Budgeted expense £	Actual expense incurred £	Adverse/ Favourable
Raw materials	16,350	17,950	Adverse ▽
Wages	12,725	11,925	Favourable ▽

(ii) Identify whether the following statement is true or false by using the tick boxes below. **(1 mark)**

Statement	True	False
A company that has a favourable variance on sales has received less income than budgeted.		X

(b) Complete the table below to show the variance and actual expense, and identify whether the variance was adverse or favourable. **(3 marks)**

	Budgeted expense £	Variance £	Adverse/ Favourable	Actual expense £
IT operational costs	13,600	680	Favourable ▽	12,920

Variance = 5% of budget = 5% × £13,600 = £680
As the cost is 5% below the budget, then the actual cost must have been £13,600 − £680 = £12,920.
If costs are less than expected, this is a favourable variance.

TASK 1.10

(a) **(i)** Calculate the variance on quality control costs. **(1 mark)**

£ | 11,300 |

(ii) Calculate the percentage quality control costs variance to TWO decimal places. **(1 mark)**

| 7.69 | %

Percentage variance = variance/budget x 100 = 11,300/13,600 x 100 = 7.69%

(iii) Identify whether the variance is favourable or adverse using the drop-down list. **(1 mark)**

| Favourable ▽ |

(b) Complete the table below to show each variance percentage. Identify whether the variance is significant or not, and who (if anyone) the information should be reported to. **(9 marks)**

	Budgeted income/ expense £	Actual income/ expense incurred £	Variance £	Variance as percentage of budget %	Significant/ not significant	Report to
Sales	150,000	166,000	16,000	10.67	Significant	Manager
Telephone	4,600	5,025	425	9.24	Not significant	Not required
Production wages	125,200	148,800	23,600	18.85	Significant	Director